# DB2 for
# Windows NT® – Fast

Springer
*London
Berlin
Heidelberg
New York
Barcelona
Budapest
Hong Kong
Milan
Paris
Santa Clara
Singapore
Tokyo*

# DB2 for Windows NT® – Fast

Mark Whitehorn and Mary Whitehorn

Springer

Mark Whitehorn
Department of Applied Computing, University of Dundee,
Dundee DD1 4HN, UK

Mary Whitehorn
PenguinSoft Ltd,
Dundee


ISBN 3-540-76200-0 Springer-Verlag Berlin Heidelberg New York

**British Library Cataloguing in Publication Data**
Whitehorn, Mark
  DB2 for Windows NT fast
  1.DB2 (Computer file)
  I.Title II.Whitehorn, Mary
  005.7'565
  ISBN 3540762000

**Library of Congress Cataloging-in-Publication Data**
Whitehorn, Mark, 1953-
    DB2 for Windows NT - fast / Mark Whitehorn and Mary Whitehorn
      p.    cm.
    Includes index.
    ISBN 3-540-76200-0 (pbk. : alk. paper)
    1. IBM Database 2. 2. Microsoft Windows NT. I. Whitehorn, Mary,
1959-  . II. Title.
QA76.9.D3W483   1997
005.75'85--dc21                                                                             97-37822

Apart from any fair dealing for the purposes of research or private study, or criticism or review, as permitted under the Copyright, Designs and Patents Act 1988, this publication may only be reproduced, stored or transmitted, in any form or by any means, with the prior permission in writing of the publishers, or in the case of reprographic reproduction in accordance with the terms of licences issued by the Copyright Licensing Agency. Enquiries concerning reproduction outside those terms should be sent to the publishers.

© Springer-Verlag London Limited 1998
Printed in Great Britain

Windows NT is a registered trademark of Microsoft Corporation.
DB2 is a registered trademark of IBM Corporation.

The use of registered names, trademarks, etc. in this publication does not imply, even in the absence of a specific statement, that such names are exempt from the relevant laws and regulations and therefore free for general use.

The publisher makes no representation, express or implied, with regard to the accuracy of the information contained in this book and cannot accept any legal responsibility or liability for any errors or omissions that may be made.

Typeset by Ian Kingston Editorial Services, Nottingham, UK
Printed and bound by the Creative Print & Design Group (Wales), Ebbw Vale
34/3830-543210 Printed on acid-free paper

# DEDICATION

For Mrs Ma,

and for Biddle,

who would have been tickled pink.

# Acknowledgements

This book wouldn't be half the book it is without the assistance of several people.

Notable among these is Adrian Lee (IBM UK). Without Adrian's comfortingly deep understanding of DB2, the factual content of the book would have been considerably less precise. But much more than that, his enthusiastic assistance and unfailing amiability when we threw him large chunks of text to proofread in impossibly short times made it a pleasure to work with him.

Jonny Black, programmer and prawn-eater, developed all of the sample code and his is the voice that speaks to you out of the README files. He also earns a huge vote of thanks for his diligence and for the many hours put in beyond the call of duty. Remaining cheerful while grappling with umpteen programming tools for weeks on end is no mean feat.

In the early days of the project, the unstinting help of Sheila Richardson (IBM Toronto) during our visit to the Toronto site was invaluable and gave us an overview of DB2 that it would have been difficult to gain any other way. Sheila is one of those people who can attend one meeting while simultaneously (and transparently!) arranging the next one. Her drive and energy contributed much to this book.

Our grateful thanks also go to David Topping (ex-IBM UK) and Herschel Harris (IBM Toronto) for their whole-hearted support of the project, without which it would never have even left the ground.

Finally, thanks to Laing's Bar for the excellent hot strong coffee that kept us awake and writing.

*Mark Whitehorn*
*Mary Whitehorn*

# Contents

Acknowledgements  **vii**

Introduction  **1**
    What is DB2?  **1**
    Target Audience – Who Are You?  **1**
    What this Book Doesn't Do – and Why  **2**
    What this Book Does Do  **3**
    Versioning  **4**
    Layout  **5**
    Hardware  **5**
    More Help  **7**
    Disclaimer  **7**

## Part 1 – Getting Started  **9**

### Chapter 1 • Installation  **11**
    Installing DB2 on an NT Server  **11**
    Creating SAMPLE  **18**
    Brief Description of SAMPLE  **19**
    An Initial Test of SAMPLE (and Introduction to the Command Center)  **20**
    What You Should Find if all Has Gone Well  **25**

### Chapter 2 • The Control Center  **28**
    Systems  **29**
    Instances  **29**
    Databases  **30**
    Creating a Filter  **32**

## Contents

The Objects in a Database  **34**
Creating a Database Using the SmartGuide  **34**
Creating a Table Using the SmartGuide  **36**

### Chapter 3 • Installing a Front-End Tool to Manipulate Your Data  **39**

Background  **39**
Overview  **39**
1. Choosing Whether to Work From the Server or a Workstation  **40**
2. Choosing and Installing a Front-End  **42**
3. Installing the CAE (and Other Software)  **43**
4a. Running the CCA on a Workstation to Create an ODBC Data Source  **48**
4b. Running the CCA on a Server to Create an ODBC Data Source  **64**
5. Configuring the ODBC Data Source  **67**
6. Configuring the Front-End to Use the ODBC Data Source  **70**
7. Manipulating the Data with Your Chosen Front-End  **81**

### Chapter 4 • Client Workstations  **83**

Making a Connection from a Client Workstation to DB2  **84**
Sample Front-End Applications  **84**
We Have Not Provided...  **85**

### Chapter 5 • Tools  **89**

Non-Iconed Tools  **89**
The Iconed Tools  **91**
Approximate Groupings  **92**
Summary  **103**

### Chapter 6 • Creating Databases and Tables  **104**

Containers and Table Spaces  **105**
Summary so Far  **112**
Why You Want to Know All of This  **114**

Creating a Database **115**
Summary **125**

## Chapter 7 • Integrity and Indexes **126**

Primary Constraints (Referential Integrity) **126**
Other Types of Integrity Constraint **134**
Indexes **138**

# Part 2 – Finer Control of Your Database **141**

## Chapter 8 • Users, Authorities and Privileges **143**

Users and Groups **143**
Authorities **144**
Privileges **146**
A Couple of Recommendations **148**
The Practical Bit **149**

## Chapter 9 • Schemas **154**

Creating Schemas **154**
What Use Are Schemas? **155**
Using Schemas **156**
Schema Names in Referencing Tables **156**

## Chapter 10 • Views **159**

Creating a View **160**
What Distinguishes a View From a Query? **163**
More Complex Views **163**
Summary **166**

## Chapter 11 • Backup and Recovery **167**

Backups – a Couple of Definitions **167**
A Quick Start with the SmartGuides **168**
Why Back Up? **175**
Transactions **176**
Rollback **177**

Logs  **177**
Backup Strategy  **181**

## Chapter 12 • Scheduling Tasks  **186**
Why Schedule?  **186**
Scripts  **186**
Summary  **190**

## Chapter 13 • Triggers  **191**
Trigger Terminology  **191**
Typical Usage of Before and After Triggers  **192**
More About Triggers  **193**
Create Trigger Dialog  **194**

# Part 3 – Advanced Features  **199**

## Chapter 14 • Monitoring DB2  **201**
Event Monitoring and the Event Analyzer  **201**
Setting up an Event Monitor  **202**
Snapshot Monitoring  **207**

## Chapter 15 • Performance  **216**
The Performance SmartGuide  **217**
Statistics for Improving Performance  **222**
Table Statistics  **223**
Index Statistics  **223**
Share Level  **224**
Recommendations  **224**

## Chapter 16 • Visual Explain Explained  **225**
Visual Explain  **225**
Running Visual Explain  **226**

## Chapter 17 • Logs  **230**

## Chapter 18 • Relational Extenders    231

Extended Data Types    **231**
User-Defined Distinct Types    **232**
User-Defined Functions    **232**

## Chapter 19 • Test Data    234

Generation Within Access    **234**
Generation Using a Front-End to Drive DB2    **234**
Importing, Exporting and Loading Data    **235**

## Index    237

# Introduction

## What is DB2?

What is DB2? This may seem a strange question, but we know people who have come in to work one morning to find a product like DB2 sitting in a box on their desk with a note saying 'Use this'. This form of 'rapid promotion' is not uncommon. We know of two other people who discovered one morning that they were network managers. In both cases they made the mistake of not being present at the meeting when the job was allocated. So it is just possible that you have suddenly found yourself responsible for DB2 and are reading this book in a bookstore at lunchtime, trying to find out about your new responsibilities.

DB2 is a database management system (DBMS); that is, it is a tool for manipulating large sets of data such as might be used by a company. In fact, DB2 is an RDBMS. The 'R' signifies 'Relational', which is simply a particular way of structuring data. Since the relational model of organizing data is not only very common but also generally held to be the best available, this is very good news.

DB2 is also a back-end or client–server RDBMS (we use the terms back-end and client–server interchangeably). A PC running an RDBMS keeps everything on the local PC: the data, the front-end and the data processing engine. A client–server system uses a server for running the data processing engine (DB2) and storing the data. The front-end is run on the client or workstation (again, we use these terms interchangeably). The front-end generates queries in SQL; these are sent to the back-end, which queries and/or updates the database and returns the result to the front-end.

*❝ Whenever we use 'DB2' in the text, what we really mean (unless otherwise qualified) is 'DB2 Universal Database Version 5 for NT'. 'DB2' just happens to be easier to type and faster to read.* ❞

## Target Audience – Who Are You?

Let's start with an easier question, who aren't you? You aren't an experienced user of DB2 for NT looking for a book which details all those

## Introduction

difficult-to-find tweaks that aren't in the manual. At least, you may well be that person, but if so, this isn't the book for you. This book is intended to allow the reader to get started with DB2 as rapidly as possible. So it doesn't tell you about that weird and wonderful tuning tip which will make your database run 3% faster on a Tuesday. Instead it tells you how to install DB2 and how to set up ODBC data sources so a client can access a database. It also defines all the terms that are reasonably common to client–server RDBMSs (such as schemas, triggers and table spaces). We have tried not only to define them but also to explain what they are used for and why you need to know about them. Finally, we have shown you how they are implemented.

By the time you have read this book, you should be able to install DB2, create a database, manipulate the data therein, connect users and backup (and restore) the data. You should be able to create views and triggers. You should also know about schemas, scheduling, users and authorities, and monitoring. In other words, you should be able to get started with DB2 quickly. At the end of the book we do stray into the rather more exotic territory of extenders and user-defined functions, simply because these are fascinating areas and you may well want to investigate them in more detail.

So to finally answer the question 'who are you?', you might be someone who is:

- moving up into the client–server RDBMS world from the PC world (Access, Approach, Paradox and the like) and need to understand the new terms and concepts;
- already using DB2 on another platform but with no experience of an RDBMS running under Windows NT or of a GUI-driven version of DB2;
- using another client–server system, such as Oracle, Sybase or Informix;
- interested in finding out about DB2 Version 5 before buying it – for example, how convincing is the GUI? How easy is it to drive?

Incidentally, DB2 has several specific names for people who can drive a DB2 server, such as SYSADM, DBADM and so on. In this book we need a generic term that describes you (as a person who wants to use DB2) and doesn't have the precise meaning that, say, SYSADM carries. We have elected to use DBA (DataBase Administrator).

## What this Book Doesn't Do – and Why

This book doesn't tell you all about the relational model. Instead, another book, called *Inside Relational Databases* (written by Mark Whitehorn and Bill Marklyn, also published by Springer Verlag) is available. This book is subtitled 'with examples in Access'. However, it is avowedly not an Access-specific book. Instead, it tries to explain the ins and outs of the relational model, and it just happens to use Access for all the screenshots. The information presented in it is vital for users of any RDBMS; nevertheless, we have chosen not to repeat it in this book for several reasons.

Firstly, many of our target readers (particularly those who are moving to DB2 from another client–server system) will already be familiar with the subjects. Secondly, having just written it all once, we had no intention of rewriting the same information in a slightly different way to try to make it sound new. Thirdly, leaving it out meant that we could make this book considerably smaller and hence considerably cheaper (sorry, more cost-effective).

However (here comes the plug), if you aren't familiar with the topics listed below, we really do recommend that you buy *Inside Relational Databases*. The book covers, among other areas:

- Table structure
- Choosing data types
- Primary keys
- Foreign keys
- Relationships and joins
- Normalization
- Integrity
- Codd's rules
- Data dictionaries (System catalogs)
- Domains
- Indexes
- Nulls

It is written in much the same style as this one, although the authors are not exactly the same. Mark co-wrote *Inside Relational Databases* with Bill Marklyn (the development manager for Access) rather than Mary. However, if you look at the acknowledgements for that book, you'll find that Mary's influence on it was highly significant.

## What this Book Does Do

The purpose of this book is to get you started with DB2 faster than you could by using only the manuals. The problem with manuals is that every entry is given equal weight. The good news is that the resulting tomes are incredibly comprehensive; the bad news is that they are massive and make it difficult for users to sort out the information that is really necessary for the task in hand. For example, take a statement like 'The table spaces in which the loaded table resides are quiesced in exclusive mode' (from p. 185 of the DB2 administrator's guide). How important is this information? Is this vital? Do you need to know it now, or can it wait until you are more familiar with the product? What is a table space, and is 'quiesce' even a verb?

We promise only to tell you stuff that we think you really need to know to get the product up and running. We will also try to give you that information in a readable way, so that when you do read the manuals you have a framework of understanding upon which to hang the information you find therein.

Incidentally, please note that we are not poking fun at the IBM manuals. We found them excellent, as we are sure you will once you get going with the product. In many ways we have a great freedom – we can pick and choose the information we give you. Manual writers are denied this freedom – they have to tell you everything – which is why manuals are so large and comprehensive.

The on-line help is good too, and an early appointment with the Information Center is well worthwhile.

❛ *The information on p. 185 of the administrator's guide is not vital when you are getting started with DB2. A table space is a receptacle for tables, and quiesce* **is** *a verb. It means 'to end a process by allowing operations to complete normally, while rejecting any new requests for work'. (We quote here from the glossary, which is another invaluable piece of IBM documentation.)* ❜

## Versioning

The release of this book was timed to coincide with the launch of DB2 Version 5. This meant that the work for it was done using beta versions of the software, and betas are, by their very nature, incomplete. We have done our utmost to ensure that the information in this book is accurate and as up-to-date as possible. However, if you should find any discrepancy between what we say and what IBM's manuals say, believe IBM by default: it's IBM's product.

❛ *We have tried to avoid repeatedly qualifying what we write with 'in the beta version' or suchlike. So, for example, when we discuss the tools, we say 'the install program creates 17 icons' rather than 'in the beta version the install program creates 17 icons, but you might see 18 if IBM decides to throw one in at the last minute'.* ❜

# Introduction

## Layout

We've been playing with applications, especially RDBMSs, for about 12 years and have found that, when presented with a new product, we approach it in the following way:

- Install it and check that it works on a basic level.
- Install any ancillaries required and check that they work.
- Organize a backup routine.
- Plunge into the detail of the product and learn by experimentation.

This is exactly the path that we outline for getting started with DB2. More specifically, we cover, among other issues:

- Installing DB2 on a server and testing
- Installing a data manipulation tool and testing
- Connecting a front-end and testing it
- Creating a database and a couple of tables
- Having a look at the tools that come with DB2
- Integrity
- Schemas
- Users and authorities
- Creating views
- Backup
- Scheduling
- Triggers
- Monitoring
- Performance

## Hardware

What you need depends on what you want to do. You can install DB2 on a standalone machine running Windows 95 or NT, but we suspect that most users will install it on a test server on a small isolated LAN with maybe one or two workstations. Isolation from any production system is highly desirable, if not essential, for several reasons:

- An isolated test-bed is ideal because you are free to play around and learn without having to worry about the requirements of other users.

- You're likely to need to down the server at various times during testing and, using such a test-bed, you can do this whenever you wish.
- Security is an important and relatively complex issue. When you first start playing around with DB2 it is comforting to know that, if you do leave any holes, people might be able to sneak in, but there is nothing sensitive for them to steal.

Memory and disk space are cheap at the moment, so buy lots of both. Speed gains from adding memory can be spectacular, and DB2 will use all the memory you give it.

IBM recommends a minimum of:

- 32 Mbyte of RAM for five concurrent users
- 48 Mbyte for 25 users
- 64 Mbyte for 50 users

We say 'Phooey'.

Our Compaq server runs NT and uses 20 Mbyte when just ticking over. With DB2 loaded that jumps to 51 Mbyte, and that's without any users connected or databases in use.

This does not mean that IBM is wrong, or lying; of course DB2 will run in 32 Mbyte. However, it will be swapping to disk and that will slow it down. If memory were still expensive we would be recommending the minimum requirements, but with prices currently around $10 per Mbyte, should you really skimp on RAM?

We recommend that, for a dedicated server, you start at 64 Mbyte and work up from there.

The number of concurrent users you expect is also a major consideration, as is the size and structure of your database. Our advice is to consult the DB2 documentation for the latest estimates (and then add a bit).

Multiple processors are also worth considering, as DB2 can make good use of these, unlike some NT applications.

A RAID array of disks is also worthwhile, because it gives a high level of minute-by-minute data security without the need for any action by you. The array in our Compaq is hot-swappable; if a disk goes bad, it can be pulled out and a new one plugged in, whereupon the transfer of data to the new disk is handled entirely automatically, and all without downing the server.

We introduce backup relatively early on in the book in an effort to persuade you that it really is a good idea, so lastly, but decidedly not leastly, you need a backup system. Even your test setup should be backed up: think how pleased you'd be if a fortnight's prototyping work disappeared in a puff of smoke.

You might be thinking, if RAID arrays are so wonderful, why you would also need to back up to something like a tape system. While a RAID array lets you carry on uninterrupted from the point of disk failure, it cannot protect you from, say, a disgruntled senior manager who spends his or her final month's notice slowly wiping out your customer table. Only a properly designed backup strategy can do this, and having the hardware to support this strategy is vital.

In case you are wondering, we do follow our own advice. We did all of the development work for this book running DB2 on a Compaq ProLiant with four processors, 384 Mbyte of RAM and a 14 Gbyte RAID array. Not only was this very fast, it was incredibly stable. OK, perhaps we became oversensitive to hardware stability while writing this book. In three months we had hard-disk failures in three (yes, really, three separate hard disk failures) of the workstations we were using (none of which were Compaqs). Very much in contrast, the Compaq server never missed a beat and we came to rely upon it entirely. If you are running a database please, for your own peace of mind, run it on fast equipment from a reputable company.

## More Help

IBM has an excellent web site at http://www.software.ibm.com/data/ for access to technical notes, white papers and all manner of interesting information.

## Disclaimer

We didn't start to finalize either the text or the screenshots used in this book until the public beta (beta 5) was released by IBM. This means that what you see in this book should map almost perfectly onto what you see in the product. Very occasionally there may be differences, but IBM assures us that these will be trivial.

No book can hope to describe how software will work under all conditions: there is too much variation in the hardware, network configurations, communications protocols, traffic loadings, how the software itself is set up and used and so on. We have researched the information for this book with due care and attention, but can take no responsibility for the actions and experiences of any reader.

*Part 1*

# Getting Started

*Chapter 1*

# Installation

You can install DB2 on an NT server, on an NT workstation and even on a Windows 95 machine. We reckon that the majority of people will be installing it on an NT server, so it is this installation that we will describe. Installation on the other systems is very similar, but if you install on one of these you might read through the IBM manual entitled *Quick Beginnings Version 5* to familiarize yourself with any differences before proceeding.

## Installing DB2 on an NT Server

The installation of DB2 for NT will come as a revelation to those used to the standard IBM installation routines. It is no longer a long-winded, unwieldy process stuffed full of deeply searching questions and guaranteed to take up days of your precious time. Instead, it is just like that of any other NT program: you are guided by dialog boxes with helpful information and default settings.

So, where do you start? Strangely, you start by ensuring that you have a user account with NT administrator privileges and a username having eight characters or fewer. Yes, we know this sounds weird, but usernames in DB2 have to be eight or fewer characters in order to provide compatibility with DB2 running on other systems. In fact, there are other restrictions besides the one on length; for example, you shouldn't use the characters / or ~, but if you stick to the usual ones (including @, #, $ and _) you should be fine. Since the install process automatically registers the installer as a DB2 System Administrator (SYSADM), the NT name of that installer has to be restricted in this way. In case you now begin to wonder (as we did) whether this means that all NT users who use DB2 have to have short names, the answer is 'no'. This restriction applies only to the installer and anyone else who is going to administer DB2.

So, the easiest thing to do is to create a new NT user with a suitably short name and assign administrator privileges to that user.

In fact, for reasons that will become clear in Chapter 8 (on authorities and privileges) we strongly recommend that you *do* create a new user and use that user only for administering DB2. We are going to side-step a detailed discussion of DB2 authorities and privileges for a while, but the following brief overview may be useful for now.

Authorities and privileges are used to control **who** can do **what** in DB2. The user you use to install DB2 will automatically acquire what is known as SYSADM (pronounced 'SYS ADAM') authority, meaning that the user can do anything and everything with DB2. This is just what you want when working with a test system, and we suggest that you continue to use the same account as you work through the book. However, remember that this user has ultimate power, not only on DB2 (by virtue of the SYSADM authority) but also on the NT server (by virtue of the administrator privileges). This shouldn't be a problem on a test server, particularly one which you back up every night (you do back up your server, don't you?) However, if the NT Server is used for other things, please be careful.

With that done, you can start the installation.

Login to the NT server as the user you have just created (we used one called Mark). You are going to have to reboot the server, so make sure you are the only user on the machine. Close all programs that are running (including those that might have autostarted without you noticing) and put the DB2 CD-ROM into the drive. The install program will then start up and you'll see the Welcome dialog. (In practice, this dialog appears, appropriately, on a background that is both big and blue; but we have removed that from the screenshot.)

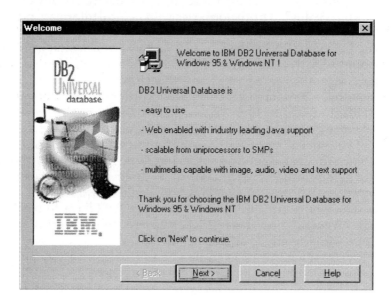

# 1 • Installation

This simply tells you how wonderful DB2 is and how wonderful you are for using it (but you knew that already). Click the Next button. A message box announces that the 'Space requirements are being calculated' after which you are asked to select the product or products you wish to install.

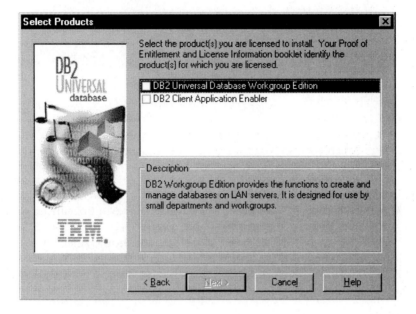

What you install will depend upon what you've bought from IBM. No matter which version of DB2 Universal Database you choose to install, the Client Application Enabler (CAE) will be installed as well, whether you actively select it or not.

The next choice is of the sort of installation you want to perform; the options are:

- Typical
- Compact
- Custom

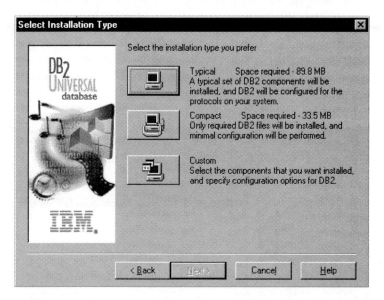

With each one comes an indication of the space required and a brief description. 'Custom' is the recommended option here, not because you will necessarily want to change anything, but simply because it allows you to see more of what is going on. In the next step, you should select everything that looks appropriate. As a general rule, if in doubt, select it. Yes, we know that it can always be added later, but then you've got to find the CD-ROM, shut down DB2, re-run the installation program....

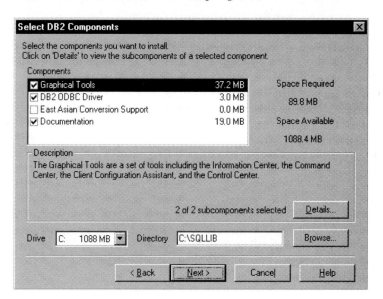

When asked whether to autostart DB2 and the Control Center, our advice is to reply 'yes' to both unless you have good reasons to choose otherwise.

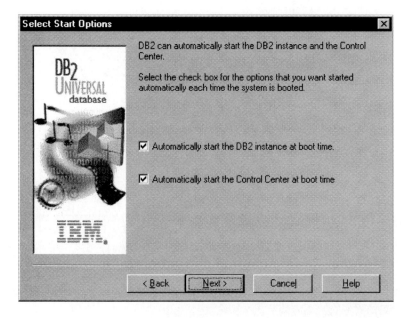

Choose a folder for DB2; the default suggestion of 'DB2 for Windows NT' is a good one.

Next comes the question of communications protocols that you can configure for the DB2 instance and Administration Server. At this point you may not know what either of these are, but it shouldn't really matter. Clicking on the Customize button for either will show you what DB2 intends to use as defaults. In our experience these are fine. However, if you use TCP/IP you might want to select DB2 Instance Customize and, in the Properties for TCP/IP, make a note of the port number, in our case 50000, because it may prove useful later.

# 1 • Installation

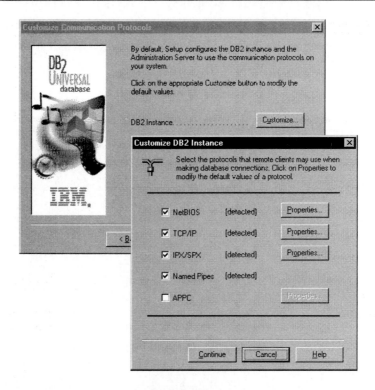

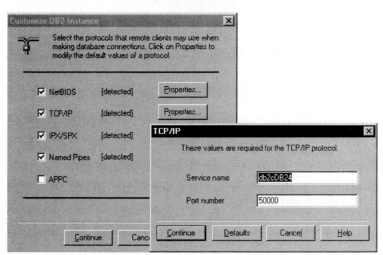

You are then asked for a username and password to enable the Administration Server to log on to the system.

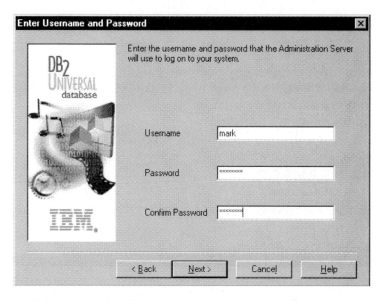

As the dialog tells you, this user must have administrator privileges, so unless you have reasons for doing otherwise, enter the details of the username and password that you're using presently for this installation.

You are then given an opportunity to review the decisions made so far, and if there is anything you wish to change, you can do so at this point. Once you're happy, click on the Install button and the install should proceed smoothly.

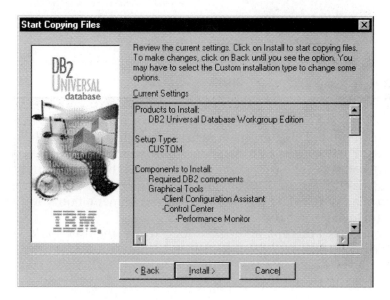

Finally, you're asked to reboot the machine, remembering to take the CD out first.

That's the server installation complete. It is very easy and mainly a case of accepting the defaults. In the course of testing different betas over a period of several months we must have installed DB2 dozens of times on several different machines. Even in beta we found the install program stable and the defaults reasonable.

## Creating SAMPLE

Once the machine reboots, it should autostart the Command Center and DB2 First Steps.

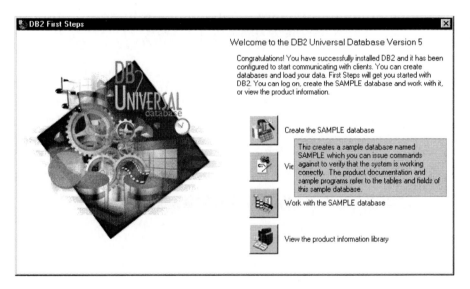

DB2 First Steps is a brief guide to DB2. It is worth investigating because it introduces you to DB2's excellent help system which includes the on-line manuals. First Steps is also the place from which you can 'Create the SAMPLE database'. We very strongly recommend that you do so. SAMPLE takes up next to no disk space (about 12 Mbyte) and, as the database is used both in our examples and those in IBM's own documentation, you will find it helpful to have on hand.

We performed this operation while logged in as the user Mark. This becomes relevant when we discuss schemas because you will see that the tables created in our copy of SAMPLE belong to the schema Mark. You should see your username appearing as the schema name in your case.

You are warned that creating SAMPLE may take some time. On a single-processor 200 MHz machine with 100 Mbyte of memory it only took a minute and a quarter. On the Compaq ProLiant it flew, taking about 18 seconds.

## Brief Description of SAMPLE

SAMPLE consists of nine tables:

- ORG
- STAFF
- DEPARTMENT
- EMPLOYEE
- EMP_ACT
- PROJECT
- EMP_PHOTO
- EMP_RESUME
- SALES

The contents are basically as you might expect – for example, ORG lists organizations:

| DEPTNUMB | DEPTNAME | MANAGER | DIVISION | LOCATION |
|---|---|---|---|---|
| 10 | Head Office | 160 | Corporate | New York |
| 15 | New England | 50 | Eastern | Boston |
| 20 | Mid Atlantic | 10 | Eastern | Washington |
| 38 | South Atlantic | 30 | Eastern | Atlanta |
| 42 | Great Lakes | 100 | Midwest | Chicago |
| 51 | Plains | 140 | Midwest | Dallas |
| 66 | Pacific | 270 | Western | San Francisco |
| 84 | Mountain | 290 | Western | Denver |

As created, the tables in SAMPLE don't have primary and foreign keys defined. Indeed, IBM is at some pains to point out that these tables are *not* meant to represent a sample database; they are just a small collection of tables that you can use for testing purposes when you first install DB2.

# An Initial Test of SAMPLE (and Introduction to the Command Center)

❝ *For those who are used to the comfortable world of the GUI, the next bit may be a shock. DB2 First Steps is about to present you with a text-based tool to test the initial installation of the database. Don't be misled into thinking this means that you will be spending most of your time driving DB2 with a command line. You can drive it that way if you want, but you can use a GUI for just about every operation covered in this book. The text-based tool just happens to be easiest way to test the installation of SAMPLE.* ❞

Once the database is created, the next step is to view it. Clicking on this option in the First Steps dialog opens the Command Center at the Script tab. The Command Center provides a text-based interface from which you can drive DB2.

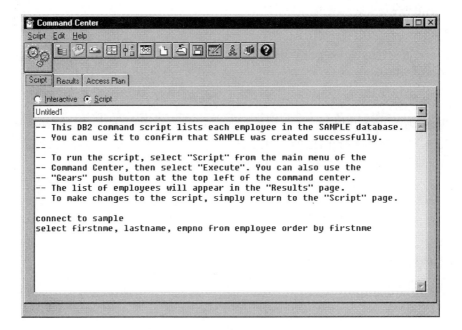

A tiny script is provided for you to test the database. All you have to do is to press the 'Gears' button (or Ctrl+Enter) and you should see

# 1 • Installation

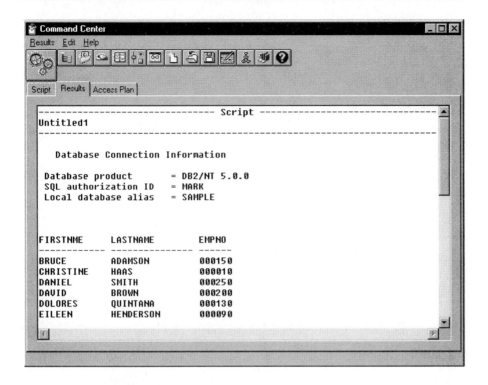

which tells you that the database is working fine. If you are used to a command line, this is also the place where you can type in raw SQL statements (and DB2 commands) to manipulate the database and view its records.

You don't have to do this next bit and, in fact, if you hate command lines we advise you not to, but you can click on the Script tab, select Interactive and connect to the database by typing:

```
connect to sample
```

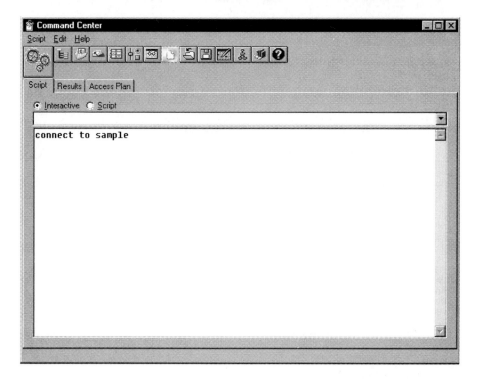

The purist's version of SQL demands a semicolon at the end of each statement, but happily DB2 is not that pedantic and you can leave it out (presumably to the chagrin of the purists). However, that group will be pleased to note that the font used by the Command Center for your SQL is the Windows System font. Since, as we all know, SQL is supposed to be written in a non-proportional font, this is an excellent choice. Joking apart, we do prefer it this way because it makes the SQL easier to read.

When you've typed in a statement, pressing Ctrl+Enter will execute that statement. You could also click on the large button with several cogs on it (its hover help – what you see when you leave the mouse pointer over the button for a short while – reads 'Start or stop execution').

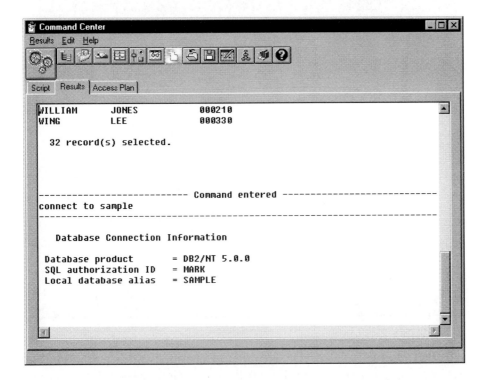

DB2 shows you the results of executing that statement under the Results tab, showing the statement followed by the output.

Click on the Script tab so that you can type in another command. For instance:

```
list tables
```

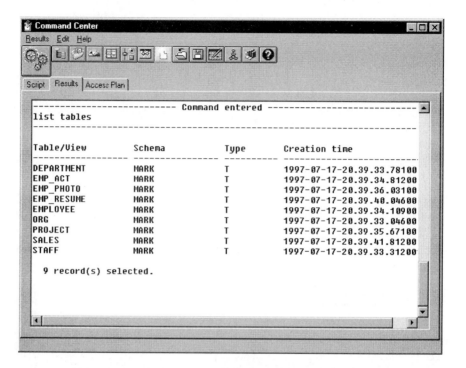

If you should mistype part of a command, click on the down arrow in the bar just above the script window. A list of previously issued commands pops down. From this you can select the one you mistyped and edit it before executing it again.

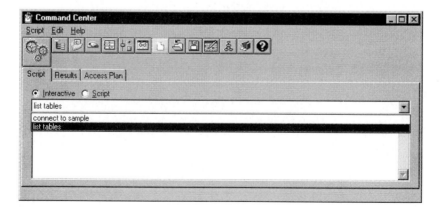

Those who are confirmed command line addicts, and who already know how to drive DB2 like this, will be in their element at this point. To them the Command Center will be the natural way to interact with the product. Nevertheless, we'll concentrate on the GUI way of controlling the product. This isn't because we think there is anything wrong with command lines (if pressed we will admit to using several), but because the GUI is new to DB2 and we feel that it is the GUI, more than any other feature, that opens up the product to so many new people.

So you can continue playing with this process to hone your SQL skills, but if you've made a connection and found that `list` and `select` work, you've already achieved the major goal, which is to verify that the database exists and that the DB2 engine is running.

## What You Should Find if all Has Gone Well

Hopefully you have installed DB2 and the SAMPLE database successfully. It is probably worth summarizing the changes that are made to your server when DB2 is installed and what you should now find running on it. That way, if for any reason your installation fails, you can compare what you actually have with what you should have in an effort to track down the likely cause of the failure.

The installation of DB2 itself creates two directories off the root – `C:\Sqllib` and `C:\Db2log`.

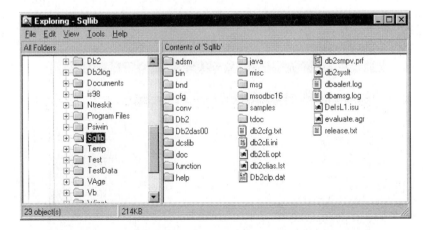

DB2 itself is located inside the maze of sub-folders that lurk under `Sqllib`. This installation takes up something under 100 Mbyte of disk space.

All that `Db2log` contains is a log file called, quite reasonably, `db2.log`.

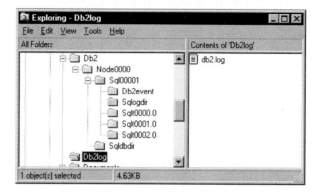

`Db2.log` records, as ASCII text, what the install program should have done and is worth consulting if anything did go wrong; otherwise you can ignore it from now on.

If you check in the Services (Start button, Settings, Control Panel, Services) you should find that two new services are running:

- DB2 – DB2
- DB2 – DB2DAS00

DB2 – DB2 is the database engine and DB2 – DB2DAS00 is the administration server that enables remote administration These are both listed for Automatic Startup.

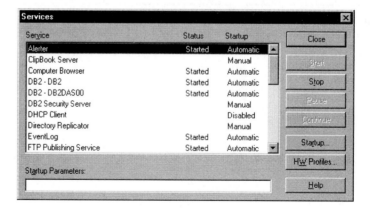

A third service, called DB2 Security Server, is, by default, not started and is left for manual startup. This service is required if certain types of authentication are used in DB2, and although it isn't strictly necessary, several IBM people suggested to us that it was better to set this for automatic startup as well unless you are sure you don't need it.

To set startup to automatic, double click on the name of the service and select Automatic. It should start all by itself the next time the machine is restarted.

If you choose to install the sample database, it will be placed in a folder called Db2, which is also hung off the root directory.

If the system doesn't appear to work and you can't find any of these folders, try re-running the installation program. Happily, we found it to be a robust process that worked well whenever we used it.

*Chapter 2*

# The Control Center

In addition to the Command Center, a full install of DB2 gives you a whole host of other tools. We were very tempted to enumerate them here, but we finally decided that you were probably keen to get on and do productive things with DB2 rather than run through all of the tools. However, it is worth introducing you to the one that you'll be using most frequently – the Control Center. So we'll do that now and leave the rest for Chapter 5, which you are, of course, free to read now if we have stimulated your interest in the other tools!

The Control Center can be found by following:

Start, Programs, DB2 for Windows NT, Administration Tools

and looks something like this when you open it up.

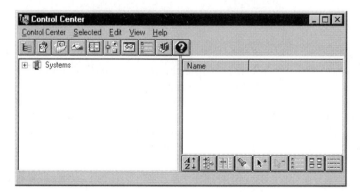

The + symbol next to the Systems shown in the left-hand window may well attract the attention of your mouse cursor. Sure enough, a click expands it to show more detail in both sides of the window. The left side of the window is known as the object tree and uses icons to represent servers, databases and the objects (like tables) associated with them. The right-hand pane is called the contents pane and displays the contents of the object selected in the object tree.

We recommend that you take a few minutes to wander around the Control Center and get a feel for how it works.

For general information, the buttons in the Control Center toolbar along the top

allow you to reach the other DB2 tools mentioned (very briefly) above.

The buttons in the toolbar below the contents pane:

allow you to manipulate the view of the objects that appear in the contents pane.

The following background information may also help to put the objects appearing in the Control Center into perspective.

## Systems

When you start playing with DB2, you are likely to be running it as a test system on a single machine. That machine may be standalone or it may be a test server on a small LAN. In either of these cases, you will see only a single System in the Control Center. This may be named 'Local' or be known by another name (in our case MW, the name of the NT Server).

If you are connected to a bigger network, other DB2 servers may be visible to your server. If so, they will appear in addition to the one you have just installed. So, in other words, the systems that show up in the Control Center are simply DB2 servers.

❦ *It is possible that there may be DB2 servers on your network that you can't see. This will be a result of the way in which they have been configured and you will have to talk to the DBA on that server if you want to access it.* ❧

## Instances

Any machine that can run DB2 can be used to manage databases. However, it is possible to run multiple copies (or instances) of DB2 on the same server at the same time. This isn't done just so that you can run more than one database on a server since a single instance of DB2 is perfectly capable of managing multiple databases. The advantage of running multiple instances on the same machine is that the different instances are essentially completely independent and isolated from each other.

Suppose you had a single NT server and used it to run, say, both an accounts database and an ordering database for your company. It would be perfectly possible to run these as two databases within a single instance of DB2.

Now suppose you wanted to develop a third database for the shipping section of the same company. You could create this new database in the instance of DB2 in which the other two databases were running and do all the development work there. However, suppose that, while developing the new database, you accidentally wrote some code that soaked up most of the resources of that instance. It would be very unlikely to crash the instance, but the other databases might start running like molasses, in which case you could reasonably expect your popularity to suffer. If you create a new instance of DB2 and do the development work in there, your established systems should be safe from the vagaries of the developing one.

Instances can also be configured. If you had several databases that were mainly used for transaction processing, you might put them in one instance. You could then use a differently configured instance for the databases that were used for decision support.

So, as a general rule, multiple instances of DB2 are used to provide a greater level of isolation between databases.

## Databases

(This definition is provided here really only for completeness. If you don't know what a database is by this stage of the book then something is seriously wrong.)

A database is a collection of related data and other components, such as indexes. The data is held in one or more tables. Each instance of DB2 can manage one or more databases.

As we have said, the Control Center is one of the main tools that you will use to drive DB2, that is, to manipulate the objects that DB2 contains. In order to see what you can do with any given object, simply right-click on it and a menu appears which lists the operations appropriate for that type of object.

## 2 • The Control Center

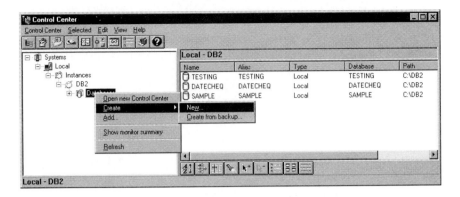

Once you are happy with the overall way in which the Control Center works, drill down to the tables in the SAMPLE database like this:

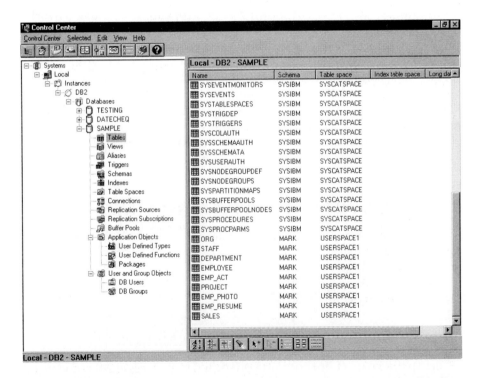

When you highlight the tables you will find about 40 with names beginning with SYS; these are the system tables. While they are fascinating in their own right, they are not what we want to look at immediately. If you scroll down to the bottom of the right-hand pane you should find the nine tables which contain the 'user' data (as shown above).

## 2 • The Control Center

By now, what appears on your screen should look very much like what you see in the screenshot. (The only major difference is that we have a couple of extra databases already in place – TESTING and DATECHEQ.)

## Creating a Filter

We became bored with continually scrolling down through 40-odd system tables just to be able to see the tables in which we were interested. We pointed this out to IBM during the beta test period (as, we are sure, did lots of other testers). The result is that in the final version (which you will have in front of you) there may well be a button dedicated to hiding the system tables. (You see what major contributions we beta testers make to your life!) However, in the event that it has not appeared, we have a work-around. In fact, even if there is a button, the work-around is worth following because it provides a practical illustration of using some of the features of the Control Center.

Click the second button in from the left in the Contents toolbar (the toolbar at the bottom of the contents pane) – hover help tells you that this opens a Filter. The dialog box that opens up enables you to restrict what appears in the contents pane. Since all of the system tables begin with SYS, it is a simple matter to set up a filter that shows everything except those that start in this way:

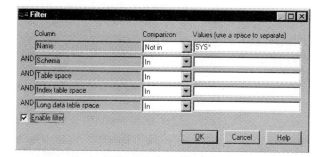

Click in the Enable filter box and you should have a less cluttered view of your data.

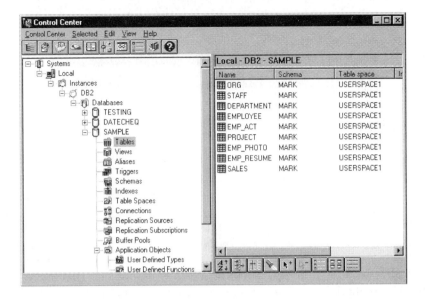

You can also practice this right-clicking business. If you select one of the tables in the contents pane, right-click on it and select Sample contents...

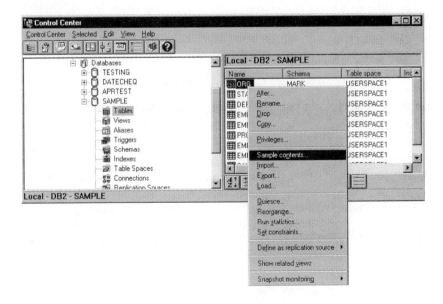

you can see what the data in the table looks like:

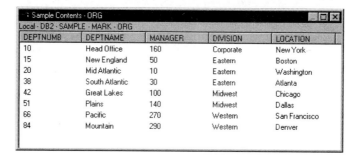

## The Objects in a Database

While you are here, it is worth having a look at the objects that are associated with a database. These are clearly shown in the object tree:

- Tables
- Views
- Aliases

...and so on

We're not suggesting that you learn them off by heart, but that you have a quick look to find out which ones already have objects associated with them (such as Tables, Views and Schemas).

## Creating a Database Using the SmartGuide

You are about to meet your first SmartGuide. These are devices that guide you through a particular process, in this case creating a database. They are very like the wizards that first appeared in Access and which have now spread to most Microsoft products. Unlike wizards, SmartGuides have tabs along the top which allow you to:

- see what is coming
- jump around the different pages more easily

DB2, like all serious back-end RDBMSs, provides a huge range of options that enable you to configure the databases you create. To produce an optimal database you will need to know things about table spaces, containers and the like (these are explained in Chapter 6) but the good news is that the SmartGuide provided by IBM for creating a database will happily choose a reasonable set of default values for you. Creating one (or several) test databases is now as easy as making fun of politicians (or falling off a log, if you prefer).

In the object tree, highlight the Databases icon, right-click and select Create, New.

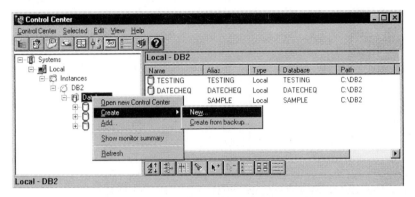

This opens up the Create Database SmartGuide. This SmartGuide has six tabs. You are obliged to fill in one piece of information on the first page (namely the New Database Name) but that's it.

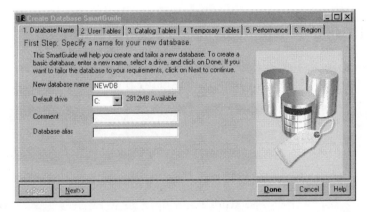

You could now click on the Done button at the bottom of that page and the SmartGuide would create a database called (in our case) NEWDB. (We get prizes for imaginative names.) But you will, of course, want to have a look at the other five tabs. We won't show them here as screenshots since we will be looking at them again in Chapter 6. (Even if you aren't very interested in the other tabs, you might want to check out the graphics!) Unless you know what you are doing, you probably won't want to actually change anything on the others, so after you have had a look, press the Done button.

Your new database should appear:

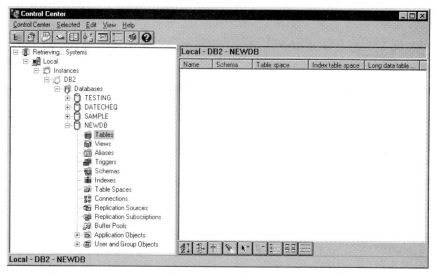

whereupon you will (presumably) be filled with an irresistible urge to create one or more tables.

## Creating a Table Using the SmartGuide

Right-click on Tables in the Object tree (making sure that you are in the right database) and select Create, Table using SmartGuide.

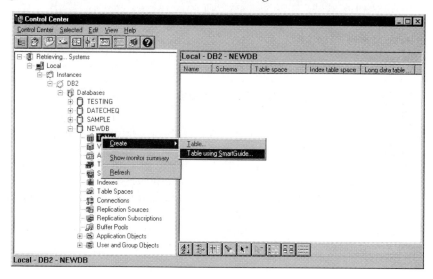

This SmartGuide has five tabs. In the first we'd advise you to enter a table name other than the default TABLENAME, but to leave the Table Schema as it is.

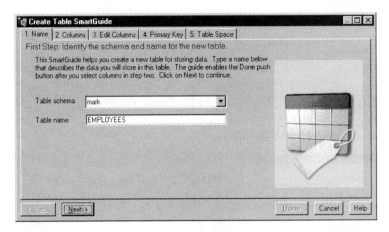

In the next page you can pick from well over 40 'column lists' which appear in the left section of the screen. As you select each one, its 'available columns' appear in the middle section of the screen, and the ones you move into the right section of the screen will become part of your table. It may not be immediately apparent, but it is perfectly possible to select columns for your table from several different column lists. In the screenshot we have chosen columns from 'Employees' and 'Money'.

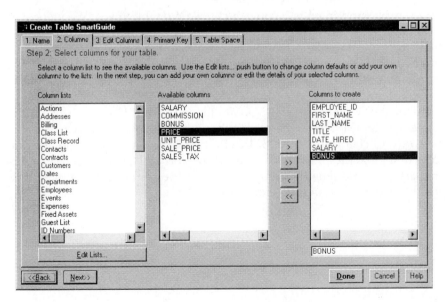

In the next page you can edit any or all of the column definitions. We'll look at this in more detail later, but note that whichever column is to be the primary key needs to be set so that it is not 'nullable'. So, in page 3, highlight the column name (in our case EMPLOYEE_ID), click on the Change button and uncheck the 'nullable' checkbox (as shown in the screenshot).

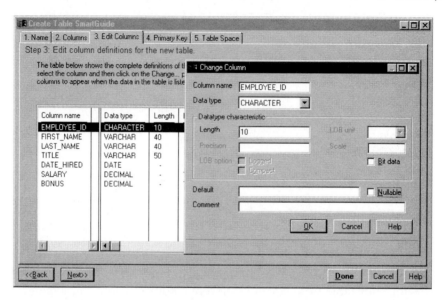

In page 4 you can choose the primary key (which is EMPLOYEE_ID in our example) and in page 5 you can choose the table space. We will cover these later, so for now you can leave these pages blank. When you click on the Done button the SmartGuide will generate the table for you.

Wonderful! You now have a new database and a table. You can, of course, play around generating several more tables just to get a feel for how the SmartGuide works.

The next obvious thing that you are likely to want to do is to add some data to the tables. This is the point where you discover (if you are new to the world of client–server RDBMSs) that DB2 has no obvious tool for that particular job. The solution is to use a front-end tool (such as Access or Approach) to manipulate the data. Setting up the connections to make this possible is described in the next chapter.

*Chapter 3*

# Installing a Front-End Tool to Manipulate Your Data

## Background

This background information is aimed primarily at people coming from a PC-type environment. People from an existing client–server environment may wish to skip to the overview section below.

DB2 is a back-end RDBMS. This means that it comes with a whole host of tools (described in Chapter 5). However, unlike applications such as Access, Approach, dBASE and Paradox, back-end RDBMSs like DB2 don't have a GUI data-manipulation tool built into them. In other words, although there are great tools for creating databases, tables and the like, there is no easy way to add data to a table, query the tables, update the data in the tables and so on. (True, we have demonstrated data manipulation with the Command Center, but it not a GUI tool.)

So, the first thing that we (the authors) do when we install a new RDBMS back-end (like DB2) is to ensure that we can connect to it with some form of GUI front-end. This gives us an easy way to play around with the data in the database. It isn't just for fun. If you are developing, say, a trigger, you need to be able to test whether it works, and the only way to do this is to alter the data in a table. As it stands at the moment, the only tool you have available for doing that is the Command Center.

## Overview

This chapter should tell you what you need to know in order to connect to DB2 and manipulate the data in the tables with a front-end tool. There are several choices that have to be made, and, since some of them interact, we end up with a huge number of different paths to achieve the same end. (You might want to use Approach to manipulate the data in three databases from a workstation, you might want to use Access from the server itself to manipulate the data in just one database... and so on.)

We can't cover all of the possibilities, but what we can do is discuss the available options and run through some of the most likely ones. The only danger from this scheme is that it might become difficult for you to follow your particular path. So here is the overall plan that everyone will follow (although not everyone will have to perform all of the steps):

1. Choose whether to work from the server or a workstation
2. Choose and install the front-end
3. Install the CAE (and other software)
4. Run the CCA to create an ODBC data source
5. Configure the ODBC data source
6. Configure the front-end to use the ODBC data source
7. Finally, manipulate the data with the front-end

(CAE and CCA are defined below.)

It is worth mentioning in passing that ODBC data sources are not unique to DB2 at all. In fact, you will probably find an ODBC Data Source Administrator (ODSA) in your NT Control Panel. An ODBC data source seems like a slightly nebulous entity on first introduction. It is essentially a description of a potential connection that can be made between a workstation and a database on a database server. What? Well, when you make use of a DB2 database from a workstation, you must have an ODBC connection between the two machines. So you first create and store a description of the connection:

- which ODBC driver it will use
- what it connects to
- who the default user is

...and so on.

Thereafter, whenever you want to make that connection, you call up the description of it rather than have to redefine it all over again. This 'description' of the connection is called the ODBC data source. Each ODBC data source is 'tied' to a particular database, and allows you to interact with the objects within that database. So if you have three databases you will need three ODBC data sources.

## 1. Choosing Whether to Work From the Server or a Workstation

Where do you intend to sit while driving DB2? Yes, we know that this is an apparently weird question, but it makes significant differences to the way in which you proceed, so it is worth thinking about now.

## 3 • Installing a Front-End Tool to Manipulate Your Data

So far we have assumed that you have been physically sitting at the server – typing on its keyboard and looking at its monitor – since this is the easiest place from which to install DB2.

It is common in larger companies for servers to be kept in a 'secure' location. These can vary from a locked broom cupboard to an environmentally controlled machine room with armed guards.

❦ *The most secure machine room we have ever seen was constructed for the Winter Olympics in Lillehammer. It was in a bomb-proof bunker hidden deep underneath one of the sports stadia. It was reached via a concealed lift shaft, and protected by passwords and some very polite gentlemen in suits who were built like hammer-throwers (perhaps they were Lille hammer-throwers?!) We were there just before the games, at which time the Norwegian government was concerned in case the games were the target of a terrorist attack (which, happily, never materialized). Since the network was only in place to support the games, we assume that room is now used to store amazingly secure brooms.* ❧

There are pros and cons in locking away a server. NetWare servers are often locked away because:

- they can be controlled remotely;
- a NetWare file server is typically only used as a file server.

NT servers can be used as servers *and* workstations, so it is possible that the machine you use as a database server will also be in use on your desk as a workstation.

So, your next step depends upon whether you intend to manage the server from its own keyboard or from a remote client across a network. Look around you. Are you in a broom cupboard? Is your neck cricked over at an uncomfortable angle because of the low ceiling and are you standing on one leg because of the brooms on the floor? If the answer is 'yes' then breath a sigh of relief, secure the server, lock the cupboard and return to your workstation.

(In practice you might have to come back to the server during this chapter, depending upon the way you choose to configure the workstation. So, if the server is *really* remote from you, skim read ahead and check out:

- Manual configuration (p. 54)
- Access profiles (p. 59)

before leaving your cupboard.)

If you are sitting in your office, with the server comfortably within reach, then you might as well drive DB2 from the server.

If you are undecided, could do either and are seeking our advice, then driving DB2 from the server is easier so go for that option.

As we said earlier, it is perfectly possible to install DB2 on a standalone machine and, if you have done that, then you will effectively be driving DB2 from the server.

## 2. Choosing and Installing a Front-End

### Choosing

We need to distinguish two different flavors of front-end tool.

One flavor (Access, Approach, Delphi etc.) comes with built-in data manipulation abilities. In other words, you can use Access to look at a table and edit the data it contains.

The second flavor (Visual Basic, C++, Delphi etc.) is, more accurately, a group of tools with which front-ends can be built. If you want 500 of your users to be able to reach data in a DB2 database, you might well write them an application in Visual Basic or C++. However, these tools usually don't have built-in data browsing tools of the kind that you require for playing around with the data during testing.

Experienced users of a tool of the second flavor may well have acquired or written toolboxes that do provide that kind of functionality. However, for those who don't already have a favorite, we recommend that you choose a tool of the first type. These tend to be PC-based DBMS products (with more or fewer relational features, depending on the product).

IBM supplies just such a front-end tool in Lotus Approach. However, Approach is not a part of DB2; it is simply a front-end tool that IBM supplies with DB2. There are many front-end tools out there in the marketplace, so you don't *have* to use Approach and, in fact, if you already have a favorite one then you will almost certainly want to use that.

On a personal level we happen to like both Access and Delphi, but clearly you should use the tool with which you are most comfortable.

❝ *Astute readers will have noticed that Delphi is described both as a front-end tool and as a development tool. Delphi is probably best known as a development tool, but Borland has added such a great set of data manipulation tools that we feel it qualifies as both. This is all a matter of opinion and degree; since Access can be used to develop standalone applications, it could be counted as a development tool as well. We don't want to offend anyone who favors any tool for any job. However, we do feel that Delphi does the best job of standing in both camps, so if you don't have a favorite tool for either job as yet, Delphi is well worth examining.* ❞

## 3 • Installing a Front-End Tool to Manipulate Your Data

### Installing

There seems little point is detailing how to install Access, Approach or any other tool you might have chosen, so we'll proceed on the assumption that you have chosen one and that you have installed it on the machine at which you intend to work.

### Background Information on the CAE and the CCA

Any workstation that is going to be used to connect to DB2 must have software installed upon it. The minimum software that it needs is the Client Application Enabler (CAE). The CAE isn't actually a program, it is a series of DLLs, so after you have installed it, don't be surprised if no icons appear on your desktop. The CAE (as the name suggests) enables applications on the client to talk to DB2.

The CAE is automatically installed on the server for you when you install DB2. In fact, when you used the Command Line Processor (which is an application) to test the SAMPLE database, it used the CAE on the server in order to talk to DB2.

You can also install the Client Configuration Assistant (CCA) on a workstation. The CCA can be used to set up and configure the links (typically ODBC) which enable a front-end to communicate with DB2.

The CCA is also automatically installed on the server for you when DB2 is installed.

A user's workstation, one that is used solely for data access to a database, only needs the CAE installed. However, your workstation, which you will use to test DB2 and play with the data it holds, needs more software installed upon it. You will almost certainly want a copy of the Control Center; in addition you may well want some or all of the documentation installed locally.

IBM supplies a setup program that installs any or all of these pieces, so that is what we are going to run next.

The setup program is located on the Client CD-ROM. (On the beta versions it was also located on the DB2 CD-ROM; your mileage may vary.)

### 3. Installing the CAE (and Other Software)

Good news for those of you who have elected to run DB2 from the server! When you installed DB2 on the server, you automatically installed all of the other bits that you'll need so you don't have to do this. You can skip this section and move to the section called 'Running the CCA on a Server to Create an ODBC Data Source' (p. 64).

## 3 • Installing a Front-End Tool to Manipulate Your Data

If you are still reading, we assume that you are at your own workstation. We are also assuming that you are using an NT workstation. You may, of course, be using another flavor of operating system on your workstation, in which case you should read the relevant section in the IBM manual called *Quick Beginnings Version 5*. However, the steps are essentially the same for all flavors of Windows.

You will need to be logged on to your workstation with a username that belongs to the Administrators group for that workstation. You should also use a username of eight characters or fewer and restricted in the same way as the user ID used to install DB2.

Pop the Client Pack CD-ROM into the drive and wait. The setup program will start automatically and the splash screen will tell you how wonderful DB2 is all over again.

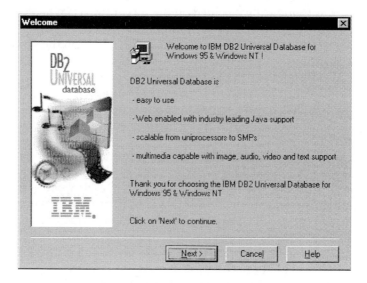

Click Next and the program checks for disk space.

## 3 • Installing a Front-End Tool to Manipulate Your Data

Then it offers you a single choice of:

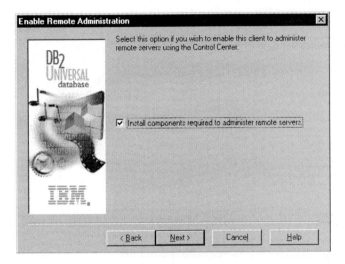

The installation program is going to give you the CAE no matter what you choose. Since you intend to administer a server you should choose the option shown. Next you are offered a choice of three options. We always choose Custom, just so that we can have a look around.

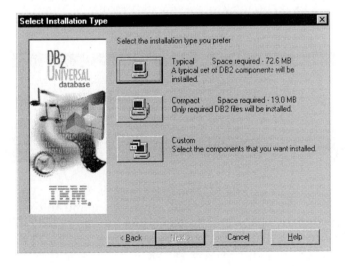

## 3 • Installing a Front-End Tool to Manipulate Your Data

The next screen shows you the components.

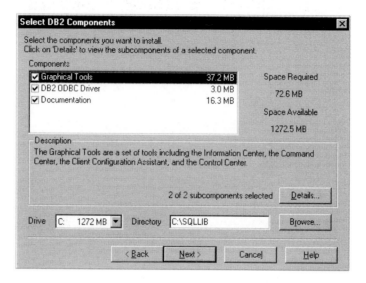

We'd recommend installing everything (as happens by default) and you can use the Details button to have a look around if you wish.

The total is a rather hefty 72.6 Mbyte, much of which is documentation. If you really can't afford the disk space then ditch some of that, but we much prefer to have a local copy if possible. The rest of the defaults (Directory and so on) are generally fine, so hit the Next button.

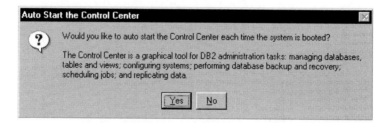

Our advice is 'Yes', you do want the Control Center to autostart, but that one's up to you. The next screen suggests that a folder called DB2 for Windows NT is created, which seems appropriate.

The one after that:

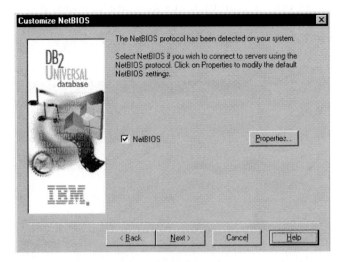

allows you to configure NetBIOS if it is detected on your system. Unless you know your way around NetBIOS, accept the defaults.

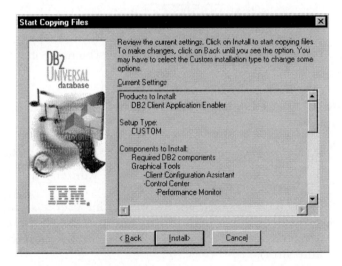

This shows a text version of your choices. Although the screen doesn't tell you, this information will be written in a file called:

C:\Db2log\db2.log

This file remains on disk after the installation is complete, which is useful to know if, at some later date, you want to check the choices you made. The

Next button will start the installation, which should proceed painlessly (it did for us every time we ran it). Once the transfer is complete, the install program is keen for you to reboot the machine, so it is probably best to let it have its own way.

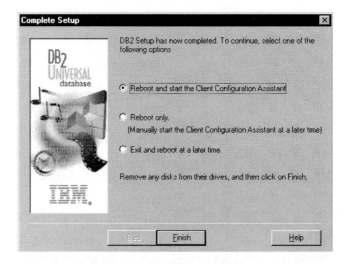

That's it. You have installed the bits you need. The next job is to run the CCA.

## 4a. Running the CCA on a Workstation to Create an ODBC Data Source

If you are using a workstation, this is the bit you need to read. If you are running on a server, skip to the section called 'Running the CCA on a Server to Create an ODBC Data Source' (p. 64).

You should just have rebooted your workstation. After rebooting, a program called the Client Configuration Assistant (CCA) will run automatically. (You can run it again at any time, of course, but the first reboot is the only time it autoruns.)

The Control Center also autostarts (which is what we asked for). However, somewhat confusingly (at least in the beta), it opens up on top of the CCA.

Our advice is to minimize the Control Center for now, whereupon you will see this screen:

## 3 • Installing a Front-End Tool to Manipulate Your Data

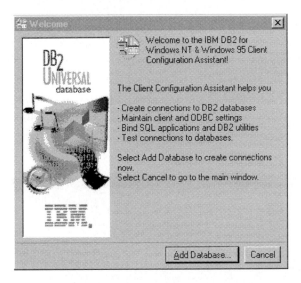

Surprisingly this one doesn't tell you how wonderful you were to buy DB2. Instead, it invites you to 'Add a database' in order to establish a database connection. Well, that's what we're here for, so press the button (which starts the 'Add Database' SmartGuide) and you find three choices appear.

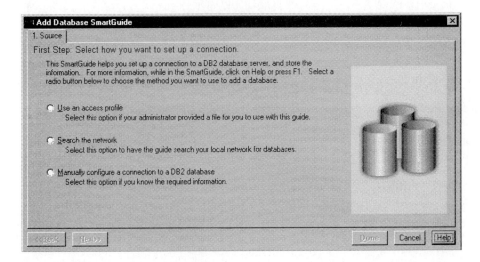

As you select the individual radio buttons, the tabs at the top of the screen vary.

- Searching the network is fine so long as the network is small. On a big network searching can be very slow.

## 3 • Installing a Front-End Tool to Manipulate Your Data

- Manual configuration is good so long as you know the required information.
- Access profiles are a very efficient way of setting up clients (your own workstation as well as those for other people).

We don't know which of these you are likely to use, so we'll demonstrate all three – but don't feel you have to try them all: one will be fine.

### Searching

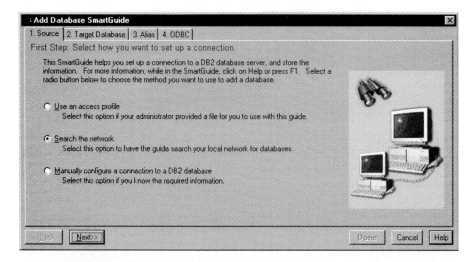

From the next screen

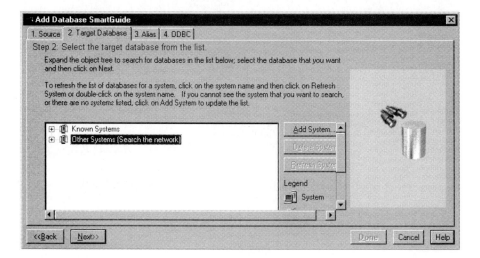

## 3 • Installing a Front-End Tool to Manipulate Your Data

select Other Systems (Search the network) and you should be rewarded with a list of servers. (This can take some time. As we said, searching the network can be slow and, given a large one, this is where you may want to go for a cup of coffee.) If you know there's a database out there but the search doesn't find it, check that the Administration Server is running on that machine; it's called DB2DAS00 and should start automatically.

Our test network has only the one server, called MW. Expand the tree (using the + symbols) to find the list of databases and choose one. We've elected to pick the old dependable SAMPLE.

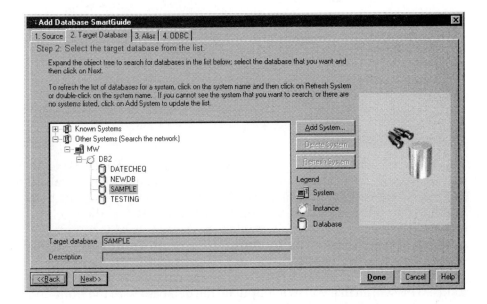

Highlight it and press Next.

# 3 • Installing a Front-End Tool to Manipulate Your Data

In the next screen you are asked for an alias.

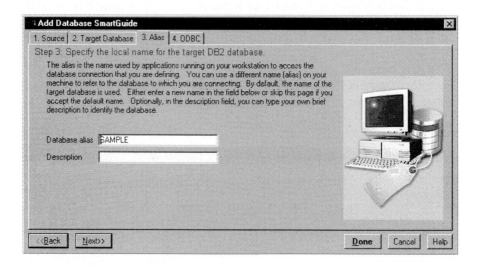

As the word 'alias' suggests, this allows you to use a different name for the database on the local machine. Here we are connecting to the database SAMPLE. If we supply an alias at this point (for example, SIMON) then SAMPLE will still be known as SAMPLE on the server, but on the workstation it will be known as SIMON. In many cases this simply adds complexity, so our advice is not to provide an alias unless you can see a benefit. In this case we'll stick with SAMPLE.

Next, you are asked if you want to register the database as an ODBC data source. This will enable you to manipulate the database with the front-end of your choice (which is the whole point of this exercise) so make sure the check box is ticked, which it is by default. If you are the sole user of your workstation, it is immaterial whether you choose 'user data source' or 'system data source'. If there are other users (apart from your current username on the workstation) then choosing 'system data source' will allow those users to reach the data in SAMPLE (assuming that they also have a username for DB2 with the correct permissions).

Finally, if your chosen front-end is listed in the Application combo-box then selecting it should give an optimized ODBC driver. If you can't find the front-end you crave then select default. We're going to be using Access most of the time, so we'll choose that.

### 3 • Installing a Front-End Tool to Manipulate Your Data

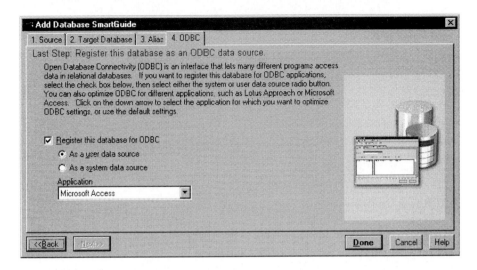

Next a small dialog box appears which (hopefully) tells you that the connection for SAMPLE was added successfully.

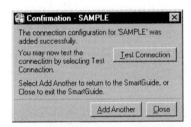

You are asked if you want to test the connection, and surely only someone with zero (not to say negative) curiosity would refuse.

Now you are asked for a user ID and password for the server. The most obvious user ID to use during initial testing is the same one that you used on the server for the installation of DB2.

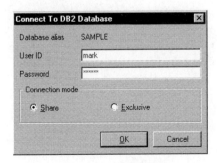

## 3 • Installing a Front-End Tool to Manipulate Your Data

As you can see, all was well in our case.

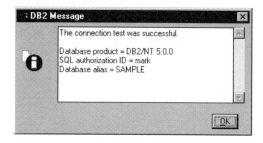

At this point you can add another database or exit the 'Add Database' SmartGuide. Typically you would exit here and try to connect from the front-end application.

What we will do is run through the SmartGuide and add another database. This time we'll do the Manual Configuration (the one where you need to know some of the information) and we'll also define an alias so that you can see what happens when one is used. At this point, if you have used the search method and have successfully added a database, you are probably really keen to see if your front-end will connect, so feel free to skip to the section called 'Configuring the ODBC data source' (p. 67) if you want to.

### Manual Configuration

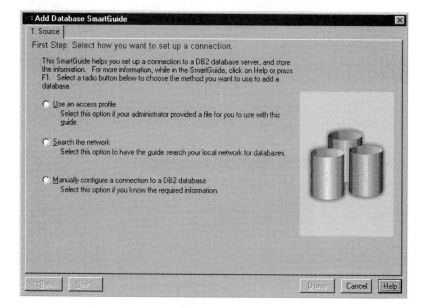

## 3 • Installing a Front-End Tool to Manipulate Your Data

Select the manual configuration option, move to the next tab and select the protocol that you are using. As soon as you do so, more tabs appear at the top of the screen. The ones you see depends upon which protocol you elect to use, so you can have fun clicking on the different options to see what appears. We use TCP/IP, so we'll demonstrate with that.

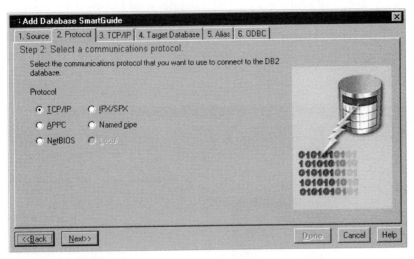

In the next screen

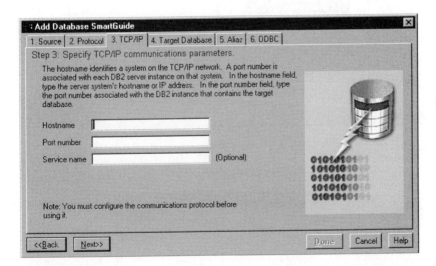

you are required to type in the HostName and Port number. The hostname is easy, since it is the name of the server you are trying to reach; in our case this is MW. The port number is the port number associated with the DB2 instance running the database we want to reach. Let's stop for a brief reality check.

We have a server called MW and an instance of DB2 called DB2. Within that instance we have several databases – SAMPLE and so on. You can probably work out easily enough that the name of the instance is DB2, but how can you possibly find out the port number?

You may have recorded it during the DB2 install on the Server. If not, it still isn't a problem so long as you know where to look. Fire up the Control Center, right-click on the appropriate instance and select 'Setup communications'.

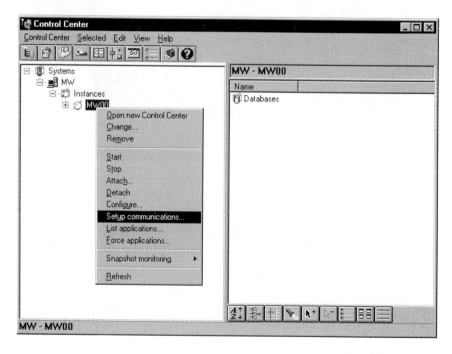

Select TCP/IP

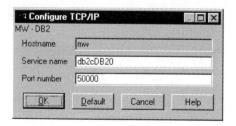

# 3 • Installing a Front-End Tool to Manipulate Your Data

and you can read the port number (in this case 50000).

Depending upon how things are set up in your case, you might have to go back to the server to run the Control Center from there, or you may be able to run it on the workstation and get the information that way. Whichever way you acquire it, you can fill in the values required for your system

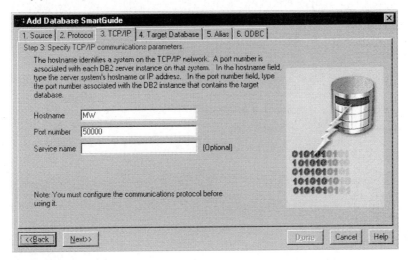

and press Next.

You will be asked for the name of the target database; we'll choose NEWDB this time, which is a database we have created within the instance DB2.

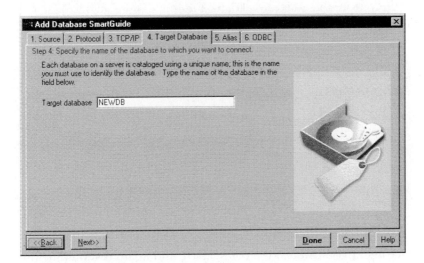

Pressing Next leads you to a screen where you can supply an alias. This time we'll supply one – KING (and also a description – Test Only).

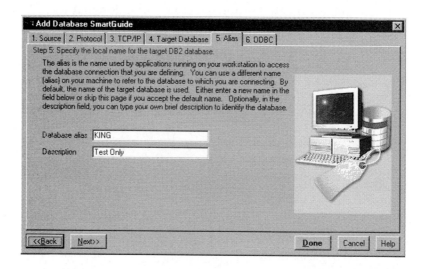

In the final screen you register the database for ODBC just as before.

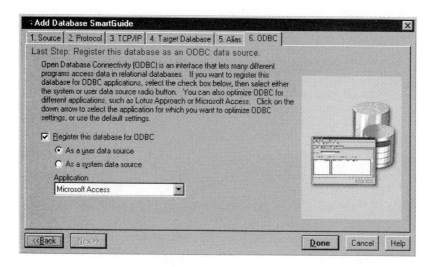

Once again you can test the connection, and again it should be fine, although it will use the alias rather than the database name.

## 3 • Installing a Front-End Tool to Manipulate Your Data

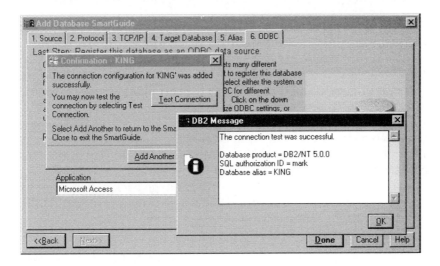

The client configuration part of the CCA shows both of our available databases.

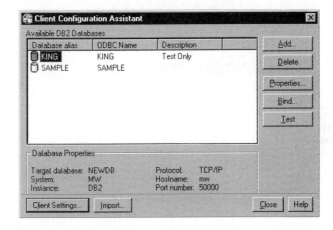

Note that we have highlighted 'KING', and you can see that the 'real' name of the database (NEWDB) appears at the bottom of the dialog box together with other interesting information.

## Access Profiles

Finally, we'll use an access profile.

If you tried the Search method described above, you may have found it slow because it has to search the network looking for information. An access profile is simply a text file generated from the Control Center containing all of the information that describes the system to which you want to connect (in our case the system called MW).

Since this information can be made explicitly available to the CCA via the text file, the search time is eliminated. Of course, you have to go through the process of generating the access profile and making it available to the client, but it is very easy to do.

In order to stop the CCA from becoming too cluttered we have removed the last two connections that were established by searching and manual configuration, so we will be starting again from scratch. This doesn't make any difference to what you have to do.

From the Control Center (and you do have to go back to the server to do this one), right-click on the appropriate System (in our case Local; in your case this may be the name of your server)

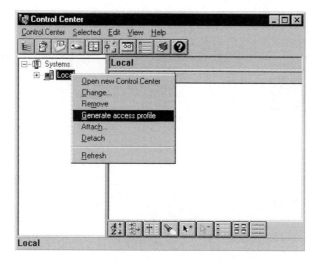

and select Generate access profile. This opens up a dialog box in which you can provide a name for the file and choose a drive and directory. Let's assume that you decide to call the file ACCPROF.TXT. Obvious choices for the location are C:\Sqllib (assuming that you can see that directory from the workstation, or A:\ if you want to carry a floppy around). It's entirely up to you. We'll elect to put it in C:\Sqllib.

## 3 • Installing a Front-End Tool to Manipulate Your Data

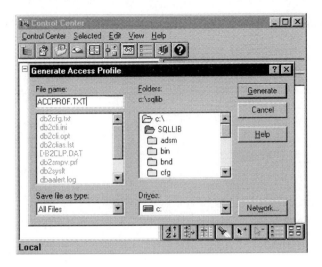

Purely out of vulgar curiosity (in other words, you don't have to do this) you can inspect this file and discover that it looks something like this:

Now back at the workstation, you select 'Use an access profile' from the first page:

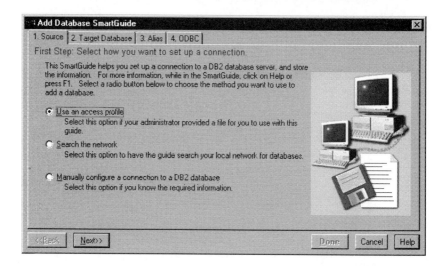

and then browse to the access profile, whereupon a list of databases appears and you can choose the one you want.

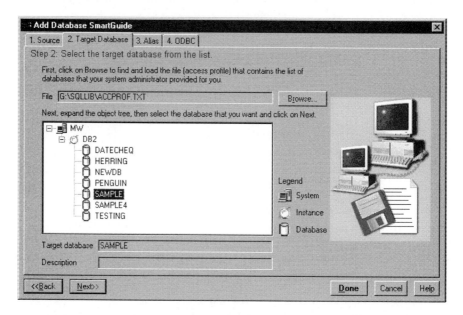

(Note that we have been adding a few databases in the meantime; you will probably only see SAMPLE at this point) Select SAMPLE, as we have done in the screenshot above, and press the Next button if you want to use an alias (see the section 'Manual Configuration' above, p. 54). If not, move directly to the last page (ODBC) and select your preferred application.

Finally, click on the Done button and test as described above (in the section 'Searching' (p. 53).

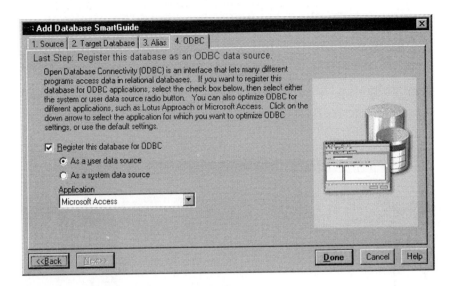

## Summary of Running the CCA on a Workstation

You have defined one or more ODBC data source(s) that your workstation can use on a DB2 server. (We say one or more; it simply depends on how many of the three options described above you tried out.) Each ODBC data source allows some type of front-end on the workstation (say Access or Approach) to access a single database on the server. For many people, especially users, a single ODBC data source may well be enough, since they will only want to access one database (and that single data source will allow them to reach all of the tables in the database). You, however, may well want to have more than one data source because you will want or need to control multiple databases.

There is some configuring of the ODBC data source that you can do, and you will of course want to see if you can actually use the data source from Access, Approach or your preferred front-end. But first we have to cover running the CCA on the server. If you don't need to do this, skip to the next section, 'Configuring the ODBC Data Source' (p. 67).

## 3 • Installing a Front-End Tool to Manipulate Your Data

### 4b. Running the CCA on a Server to Create an ODBC Data Source

If you are sitting at the server, you should have skipped to here. If you are using a workstation then skip to 'Configuring the ODBC Data Source' (p. 67).

You don't need to install the CAE because it was installed at the same time as DB2. Now you need to run the CCA by choosing:

Start, Programs, DB2 for Windows NT, Client Configuration Assistant

whereupon you should see it running like this:

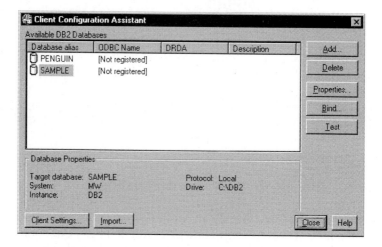

The database(s) that you have created should be visible, but not registered (which effectively means you can't use them from a front-end yet). Highlight SAMPLE as shown and press Properties. This dialog box opens up:

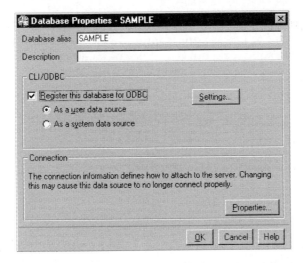

You can, at this point, provide an alias for the database. Our advice is not to bother for the moment. This feature is more useful when connecting from a workstation.

Select Register this database for ODBC (as shown). If you are the sole user of your server, it is immaterial whether you choose 'As a user data source' or 'As a system data source'. If there are other users (apart from your current username on the server), then choosing 'As a system data source' will allow those users to reach the data in SAMPLE (assuming that they also have a username for DB2 with the correct permissions). Then press Settings.

You will be asked if you want to connect to the data source. Choose Yes and enter a user ID and password (the same one you used for the install of DB2). You should be told that the connection was completed successfully. Click on OK and you should see a dialog box like this one:

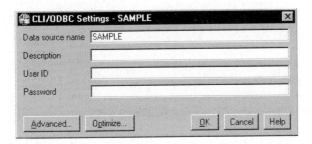

You might be tempted to fill in a username and password here, but our advice is don't. Wait until you have read the section called 'Configuring the

ODBC Data Source' (p. 67). Click on Optimize and choose the application which you intend to use as your front-end. If it isn't listed then the ODBC data source will still work, but it will not be as efficient as it might otherwise. In the screenshot below, we are choosing Access.

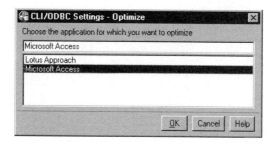

And that's it. As you close the dialog boxes, you should get a message telling you that the database list has been successfully updated. When you get back to the main screen of the CCA,

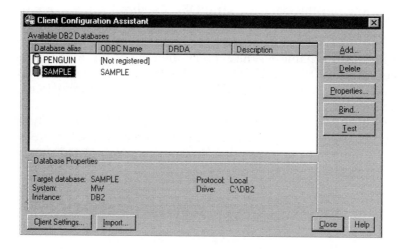

SAMPLE should be registered.

## Summary of Running the CCA on the Server

You have established one or more ODBC data source(s) which allow connection to the databases managed by DB2. (We say one or more; it simply depends on how many you have made. In the screenshots shown above we have made only one – to SAMPLE.) Each ODBC data source can provide access between some type of front-end and a single database. As the SYSADM you may well want to have more than one data source because you will want or need to control multiple databases.

There is some configuring of the ODBC data source that you can do, and you will of course want to see if you can actually use the data source from Access, Approach or your preferred front-end. That's what we will look at next.

## 5. Configuring the ODBC Data Source

Whether you are working on the server or on a workstation, you should be reading this section. You've just used the CCA to create one or more ODBC data sources. As created, these data sources should work reasonably well, but you may want to configure them, so we'll look at how that is done.

When you run the CCA, you should see something like this (the number of data sources displayed on your screen will depend upon the number you have set up).

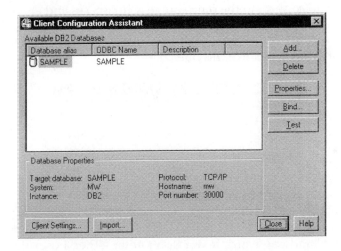

Highlight SAMPLE as shown and press Properties.

## 3 • Installing a Front-End Tool to Manipulate Your Data

This dialog box opens up:

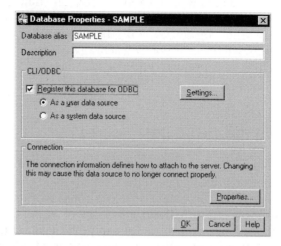

Here you can choose to make the ODBC data source available to just yourself – 'As a user data source' – or to all users of your machine – 'As a system data source'. If you now press Settings a dialog appears which asks if you want to connect to the data source. Choose Yes and enter a user ID and password (the same one you used for the install of DB2). You should be told that the connection was completed successfully. Click on OK and you should see a dialog box like this one:

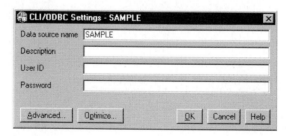

You can enter a description of the database if you wish. You can also enter a user ID and password. If you don't enter either a user ID or a password, then the ODBC data source will still be fully functional; however, every time you use it to connect to a database you will have to supply both of these pieces of information. 'Ah', you cry, 'then I'll fill these in to save myself time and effort in the future'. 'Ah', we cry, 'just before you do...'. You need to be aware that if you have made the ODBC a system data source (see paragraph above) then everyone who uses the database via this ODBC data source from this machine will be connecting under your user authority. You may not want this to be the case.

## 3 • Installing a Front-End Tool to Manipulate Your Data

Secondly, and more importantly, whichever type of data source you choose, if you type in a user ID and password, DB2 will store these, as plain unencrypted ASCII, on the local machine. In fact, they are stored in a file called db2cli.ini in C:\Sqllib. Here is an example:

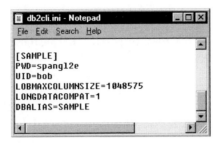

We find this a little unnerving, to say the least. It might be all right on specific, well-protected machines, and/or it might be acceptable if the user ID only had read access to non-confidential files. But as a general rule we'd steer well clear of anything that writes passwords to disk in a totally unencrypted fashion.

All of this was true in the beta. If other beta-testers also registered 'surprise' at this storage of unencrypted passwords, then perhaps it has been altered in the release product. If you are interested in this feature, you might want to check that what we found is still true; it might not be.

However, you can still have fun configuring the ODBC data source in other ways. From this dialog box:

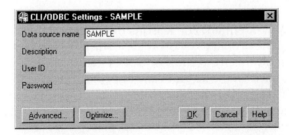

you can select Advanced and Optimize. The Advanced setting falls outside the remit of this book (but it is good to know where you can find and alter this information). Optimize allows you to optimize the data source for your chosen front-end. In fact, you should have done this already, but you can reconfigure the setting if required.

Once you are happy with the configuration of the ODBC data source, save it.

## Summary so Far

You have installed DB2 and checked that it runs. The CCA can be run on the machine from which you want to drive DB2 (the server or your own workstation) and you have used it to set up one or more ODBC data sources. You can also use the CCA to create more data sources or edit the existing ones.

You should also be able to manipulate these ODBC data sources using the ODBC Data Source Administrator (ODSA), which you should find in your NT Control Panel. Discussions of the ODSA fall outside the scope of this book, but if you are familiar with that tool you may well prefer to use it in place of the CCA. Even if you aren't familiar with it, you might find it worth investigating, since it provides the easiest GUI way of removing data sources!

Each ODBC data source is 'tied' to a particular database, and allows you to interact with the objects within that database. So if you have three databases you will need three ODBC data sources.

However, so far none of your ODBC data sources are tied to a front-end on your chosen machine. One end has been tied to a database, but the other dangles free. The next step is to tie the free end of your ODBC data source to a front-end.

## 6. Configuring the Front-End to Use the ODBC Data Source

We have said that you could be using any one of a number of front-ends, but we think the three most likely ones will be Access, Approach and Delphi, so we'll look at those.

As we have already noted, by default the tables in SAMPLE don't have their primary keys defined. For reasons that will become clear below, it is worth defining the primary key on at least one table before starting this exercise. You can do this from the Control Center. Navigate to the tables in SAMPLE, right-click on the appropriate one, pick Alter, choose the Primary Key tab and then select a sensible column to be the primary key. We recommend that you set DEPTNUMB to be the primary key in ORG, as we have done for this exercise.

### Access

We are assuming that you have created an ODBC data source called SAMPLE that allows access to the database called SAMPLE.

Start up Access and create a database.

Access defaults to naming the databases you create DB1, DB2 and so on. We couldn't resist using the second default name, for obvious reasons.

## 3 • Installing a Front-End Tool to Manipulate Your Data

At this point your Access database is empty.

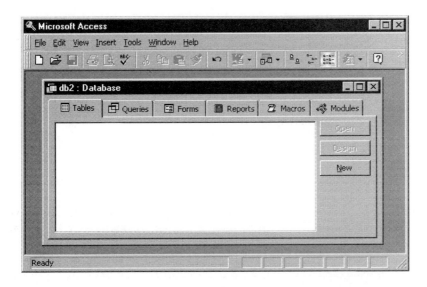

From the main Access menu select File, Get External Data and Link Tables, whereupon this dialog opens up.

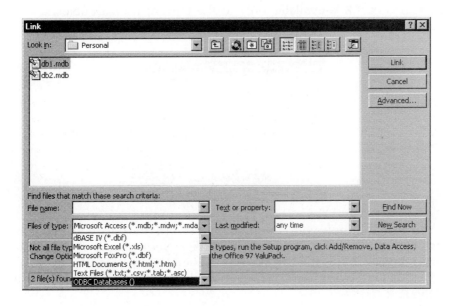

### 3 • Installing a Front-End Tool to Manipulate Your Data

Choose ODBC Databases () as shown, and when the dialog box opens, choose the Machine Data Source tab.

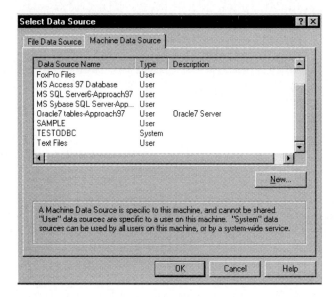

As you can see, we have two data sources defined. Both are specific to the current machine. Any user of the workstation can use TESTODBC, whereas SAMPLE is available only to the current user. Double click on SAMPLE and this dialog appears:

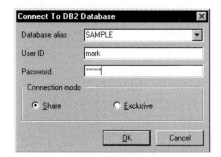

You need to supply your user ID and password (the ones you use on the server). No paranoia is required at this stage; your password will not be stored on disk in ASCII when you enter it here!

This dialog box appears, which lists all of the tables that appear in SAMPLE.

## 3 • Installing a Front-End Tool to Manipulate Your Data

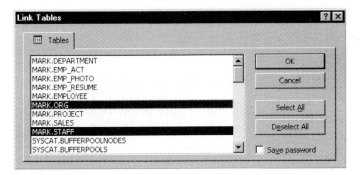

You can choose one or more, using the Windows conventions (Shift-click and Control-click). Note the check box that is labeled Save Password. This is Access, rather than DB2, offering to save your password. On principle we are against this, but it is up to you.

Access will then look at all of the tables. Assuming that each has a primary key defined within DB2, all proceeds smoothly. If any of the tables don't have a primary key, Access will ask you to choose one, as in this case.

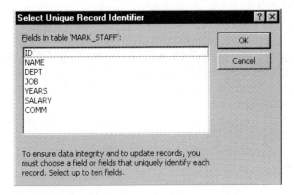

We found, by experimentation, that the little bit of text at the bottom of the screen (the bit that is so easy to overlook!) is telling the truth. If a particular table doesn't have a primary key, and you fail to identify one for Access, several operations on the table (like updating) become impossible. So this step is non-trivial and well worth completing. However, in a real database we would expect all tables to have primary keys defined within DB2, so it shouldn't matter.

Once you have finished this process for all the tables you have chosen, you can, at last, see them from within Access and you can start to manipulate them.

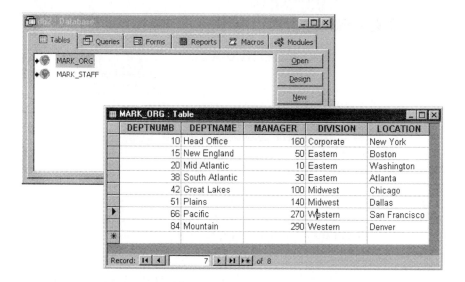

We thoroughly recommend that you spend some time here, working out what can and can't be done from within Access.

You should find that you can define joins between the tables for the purposes of querying. These joins do not enforce referential integrity between the tables, since this function falls within the remit of DB2. However, they do limit the records returned by queries.

You should also find that you can query, update and insert data in all of the standard field types – text etc.

In other words, you *can't* do most of the jobs that should be left to DB2, and you *can* use Access to perform the jobs that were difficult with DB2. It's really a rather satisfactory arrangement!

## Approach

We are assuming that you have created an ODBC data source called SAMPLE that allows access to the database called SAMPLE.

Load Approach, select the Open an Existing Approach File tab (even if you know that you haven't any) and press the Browse for More Files button.

## 3 • Installing a Front-End Tool to Manipulate Your Data

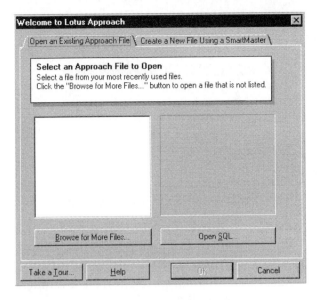

Select IBM DB2 (*) as the file type,

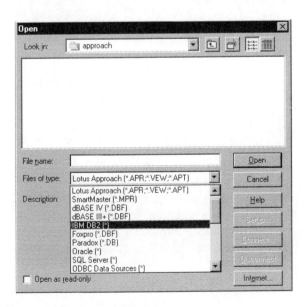

whereupon this dialog opens.

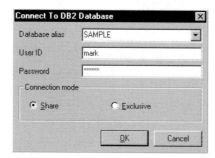

Choose the database alias you require (SAMPLE in our case), and enter the user ID and password that you use on the server (these will *not* be stored in plain ASCII on the hard disk). Click on OK and, after a brief pause, you should see something like this.

Double click on mark@db2 (or whatever your equivalent is) and a list of the schemas in the DB2 instance appears.

We haven't covered schemas in any detail yet, but they are simply a way of classifying objects in the databases. Since we created SAMPLE with the user ID Mark, the tables we want are in there. Double click on Mark (or your equivalent) and you should find the now familiar nine tables of SAMPLE.

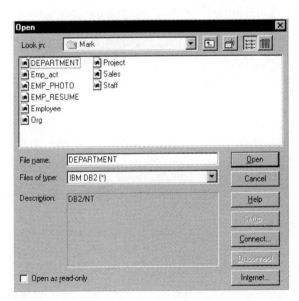

Double click on the one of your choice and it opens up. (In the screenshot we have clicked on the Worksheet 1 tab so that multiple rows are visible at the same time.)

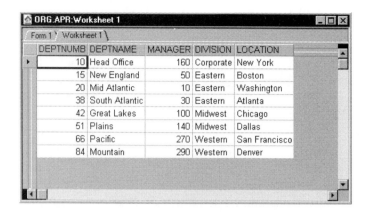

As we said above, we had already set DEPTNUMB to be the primary key of ORG. That being the case, we can edit the data that the table contains. If the table hadn't had a primary key defined in DB2, then we would be able to see, but not update, the data.

Approach offers a variety of ways of saving the work you have completed so far. The easiest option is to use File, Save Approach File rather than File, Save As... – at least for the first couple that you create.

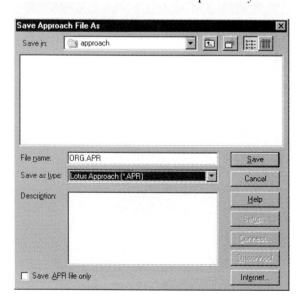

# 3 • Installing a Front-End Tool to Manipulate Your Data

Once the file is safely saved, repeat the steps described above to open a new file. As soon as you reach the stage of selecting IBM DB2 (*) as the file type, you will see the tables in SAMPLE and can choose another one.

As we said about Access, we thoroughly recommend that you spend some time here, working out what can and can't be done from within Approach. You should be able to apply your existing Approach skills to manipulating the data within the DB2 tables, manipulations which are possible but somewhat tedious with the standard DB2 tools.

## Delphi

We're presuming you'll start from a state where you've installed both the CAE and the CCA on the workstation and have used the CCA to set up an ODBC data source for accessing data within the SAMPLE database on DB2. You'll also have Delphi loaded on the workstation.

Load the Database Desktop, one of the components of Delphi. Click to pop down the Tools menu options and select Alias Manager.

Click on the New button and, in the left side of the window, fill in a database alias – this is a name to identify, within Delphi, the database to which you will attach. We've used Fred. Now select DB2 as the Driver type. When you do so, further options appear. There are only two that you must complete: one is the Username – ours is Bob – and the second is the DB2 DSN, which for us is SAMPLE.

79

## 3 • Installing a Front-End Tool to Manipulate Your Data

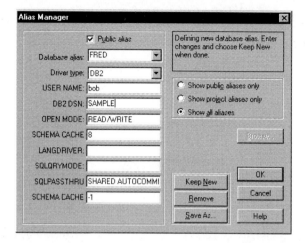

Click OK and a dialog will ask if it's OK to save under a default file name, to which we replied Yes.

Click on File, Open, Table and select the Fred alias from the list and provide your password when asked. The available tables now appear, and clicking on one selects it as the file name of the file at which you want to look.

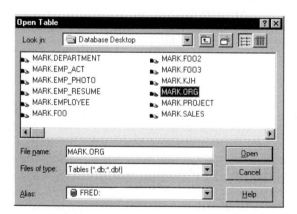

Click on Open and the table appears.

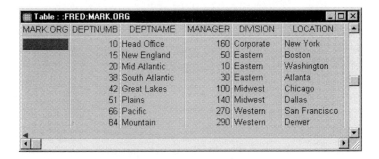

To query a table, select File, New, QBE query, select the table as before and build your query in the graphical tool provided by Delphi.

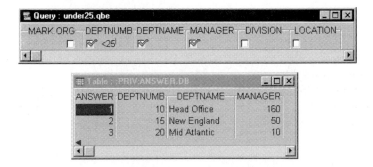

## 7. Manipulating the Data with Your Chosen Front-End

We felt it was important to outline how the most common front-ends can be connected to DB2, but we don't intend to discuss in detail how they can be used to manipulate data in DB2. For a start, this book is about DB2 rather than other products, and for another we assume that you know how to use your chosen front-end, but it is worth throwing some general ideas around.

You can, of course, simply use the front-end to type in sample data.

When we get on to things like triggers (which can, for example, detect and respond to changes in data) you can use the front-end to make such changes and thus trigger a trigger in order to see if it is working.

However, you can be slightly more imaginative. For example, when you get around to building views, you will find that you need to write SQL. Unless you enjoy hand-crafting SQL, you'll probably find it easier to use the front-end to build the relevant query, and then cut and paste the SQL from there into DB2. (This is discussed in more detail in the chapter on Views.)

Finally, suppose that you want to generate large sets of test data. You may find it easier to do this using the control language built into your favorite front-end. We certainly do, and we have provided a tool which should help – this is described in Chapter 19.

*Chapter 4*

# Client Workstations

By now you should have DB2 installed on the server and you should have managed to set things up so that you can manipulate the data from a front-end of your own choosing. From here on, you should be able to try out the work described in the following chapters, learning about DB2 as you go along.

This chapter is about creating a front-end application to DB2 for use on users' workstations. Typically, the people who build such applications are programmers, and that may or may not be you, since there is no obligation for a DBA to be a programmer. So, if you intend to administer DB2, but not build front-end applications for it, you can happily skip this chapter.

If you are still reading, we are going to assume for the rest of this chapter that you have some programming skills. In turn, this means that we are going to keep our explanations to a minimum, because we will assume that you know about README files, comments in code, directories, DOS commands and so on.

On the CD-ROM supplied with this book you will find a subdirectory called DB24NTF. It contains various subdirectories, one each for:

- Visual Basic
- VisualAge for Basic
- Delphi
- Java

We recommend that you move the sample files from the appropriate directory to your hard disk and run them from there. We have included a batch file called D:\DB24NTF\INST.BAT. This installs all of the sample files as well as the data generation tool described in Chapter 19. The batch file simply creates a directory C:\DB24NTF and puts the files into the appropriate subdirectories under that. You can either run this DOS batch file or copy the files you need across to your hard disk manually.

In order to allow users to access a database you will need:

- to make a connection from the user's workstation to DB2;
- to produce some form of front-end application that the users can run on their workstations.

## Making a Connection from a Client Workstation to DB2

Essentially, all you have to do is to read and carry out the instructions listed in Chapter 3 in the following sections:

- Running the Setup Program to Install the Software (p. 43)
- Running the CCA on a Workstation to Create an ODBC Data Source (p. 48)

Clearly the only major difference is that, in Chapter 3, we advise you to install the Control Center and all of the documentation. This was because we were describing the installation that you would carry out on your own machine. When you are performing an installation for a user's workstation you would normally install just the CAE, the CCA and a very small amount of documentation. This is all handled automatically by the client installation program as long as you make the correct selections, which are spelt out quite clearly.

## Sample Front-End Applications

We've found that making the first connection between a front-end application and something like a back-end database can be a painfully difficult step. What we did was to take four application development tools/languages:

- Visual Basic
- VisualAge for Basic
- Delphi
- Java

and mount the necessary components from each on a workstation. Then we produced a program in each which connected to DB2. These programs only allow simple manipulation of data, but they do show you how to make that all-important first connection.

At best, if you use Visual Basic, for instance, you would simply need to do the following:

- Read any relevant READMEs that you find.
- Load VB on a workstation.
- Load our sample.
- Examine the code and read any comments therein.
- Edit the code if necessary to reflect your instance names, port numbers etc.
- Run it to see if it works.

❢ *We are painfully aware that most people will ignore this advice and just run the code to see if it works or falls over. We have no objections if you do, but don't be surprised if it then falls over!* ❥

Each piece of sample code contains handling notes as appropriate. Some have associated README files, some have comments within the code and some have both. The samples are to be seen as written from one programmer to another; if you're not familiar with the language, the comments and code might not make a great deal of sense.

Delphi is an interesting exception here: no code is needed to make a connection as it is achieved by setting object properties. There is therefore no code to document, and this in turn makes the sample more difficult to understand. The readme for Delphi is quite extensive, and reading this and building a sample for yourself might help you to understand what's going on more quickly than dismantling the sample.

❢ *We are aware that some users may utilize data-manipulation tools like Access and Approach to manipulate the data. (You can, indeed, use an Access developer's toolkit to produce 'compiled' versions of front-ends that you develop with Access.) We haven't discussed these here, since establishing the connection is essentially the same as described in Chapter 3.* ❥

## We Have Not Provided…

We have been very careful to describe what we are supplying as sample programs/code, not sample applications, because these are *not* tiny applications. In other words, there is no error trapping and the samples do little more than provide a connection to DB2 and retrieve data. The lack of error trapping means that they are not crash-free applications which you can present to your users. They are samples of code, passed as from one programmer to another, which show you those vital few lines of code that you would otherwise have to hunt through various manuals to locate and tweak before establishing a connection.

Indeed, there is no guarantee that they will even work on your system; too much is outside our control. It's your system, your network and we give no guarantees.

OK – that's all of the bad news finished with. The good news is that we *are* sure that the code we supply worked on our system exactly as described here; each sample has been used many times to establish a connection to DB2. We hope it will work for you – if it doesn't, you'll at least have something to mull over and hack at until it does.

## Visual Basic

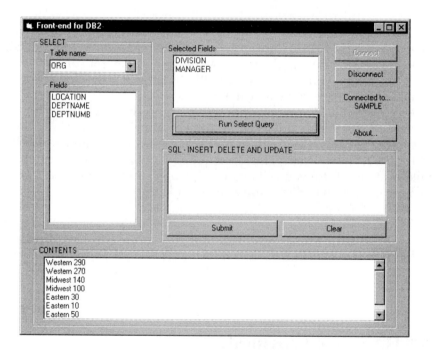

## VisualAge for Basic

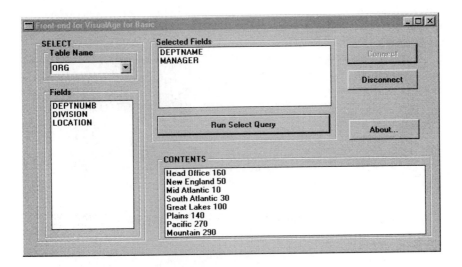

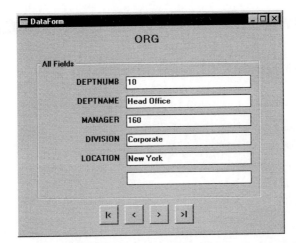

## Delphi

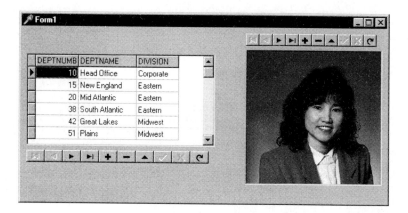

## Java

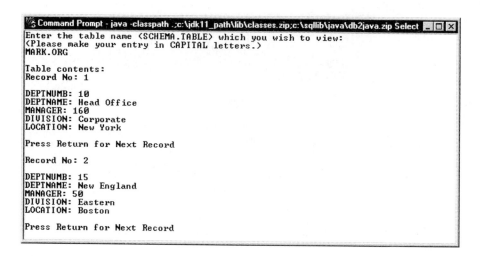

*Chapter 5*

# Tools

'The time has come', the Penguin said, 'to talk of many tools.'

By now you should have sated your desire to get the product installed and working. You can create databases, add data and manipulate it; in other words, your RDBMS is up and running. Now is the time to have a look around at the extra toys (sorry, tools) that are provided with DB2. This chapter is intended to give you an overview of all the tools. For some of them, this overview will be all the information you need to know for a fast start. Others, like the Script Center and Journal, will be described in more detail later. What we are trying to do here is to give you an overview of them all and a feeling for the way in which some of them work together.

DB2 provides a huge range of tools with which you can configure and monitor your database.

## Non-Iconed Tools

Most of the tools in DB2 can be reached via icons (as described below). There are two important ones that don't have icons and, instead, are run by right-clicking on objects in the Control Center's object tree. These are:

- Event Monitor
- Snapshot Monitor

## Event Monitoring

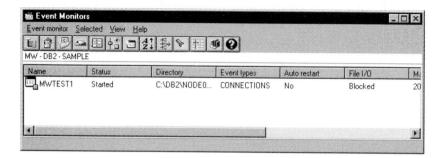

The Event Monitoring tool is used to monitor events (*no, really?*). An event is something that happens to a database – a connection to a database, a read from a table or an update to a record, for instance. You can build an event monitor that will log the occurrence of these and many other events to a file. Later study of the resulting information can help you to improve the performance of your database, among other things. Event monitors are endlessly configurable and are vital for pinpointing bottlenecks and other problems.

## Snapshot Monitoring

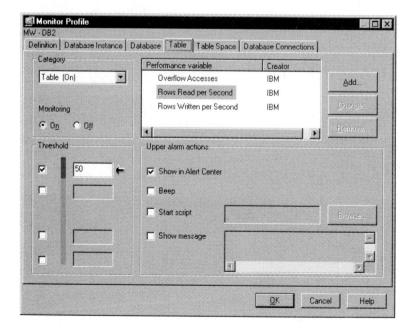

Snapshot Monitoring also collects performance data, but, rather than monitoring the situation over time, it provides information about situations as they occur. When a problem manifests itself (maybe everything starts running slowly) looking at the output from the snapshot monitor can help you to diagnose what's happening, and once you know the cause, you can look for a solution.

The difference between Event and Snapshot monitoring may not be immediately apparent, but a couple of examples may help. Suppose that you wanted to keep track of what a particular user was doing. You could use an event monitor to log every action (event) carried out by that user. You could then examine the information collected to see what the user had been doing.

On the other hand, suppose that you were concerned about the number of rows being read from a particular table, rather than who was doing the reading. In other words, you weren't concerned with any particular event (whether user X read from table `ORG`); you were only interested if the total number of rows read from `ORG` exceeded, say, 50 per second. In that case you would use Snapshot Monitor, which could, for example, make the server beep as soon as that limit was reached or exceeded.

Both monitoring tools are covered in more detail in Chapter 14.

## The Iconed Tools

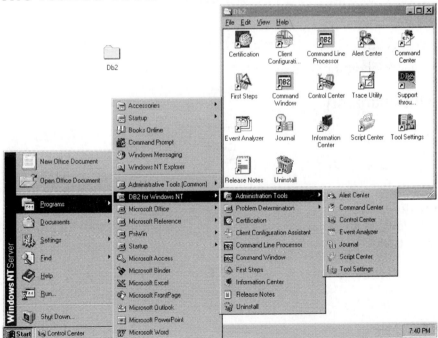

You will find that the DB2 installation program throws out 17 tool icons, and these are typically found under:

- Start, Programs, DB2 for Windows NT
- Start, Programs, DB2 for Windows NT, Administration Tools
- Start, Programs, DB2 for Windows NT, Problem Determination

We found it helpful to put short cuts to all these tools into a folder called DB2, but you can configure it as you wish.

## Approximate Groupings

These tools are apparently ungrouped, but we found that, as we worked with them, several logical groupings emerged. We'll organize the tools into these 'unofficial' groups as we discuss them.

### Already Covered

First Steps    Client Configuration Assistant

The following two have already been covered:

- First Steps
- Client Configuration Assistant

### Self-Explanatory

Uninstall

- Uninstall

You don't really need us to explain this one, surely?

### Obscure

Trace

- Trace Utility

This one can be ignored in this discussion because, as the manual says, 'use the trace facility only when directed to do so by an IBM Support Center Representative'. In other words, they'll tell you if you need it and tell you how to use it.

## Information

Certification

Support through Internet

Release Notes

Three of the tools simply provide a route to further information, and are:

- Certification
- Support through Internet
- Release Notes

## Propeller-Head

Command Line Processor

Command Window

- Command Line Processor
- Command Window

These two are worth some discussion; feedback received by the IBM User Centered Design team showed that users had problems differentiating between them. Part of the confusion stems from the fact that they are very similar in appearance and have very similar names. (*Put like that, is it any wonder that people confuse them?*)

### Command Line Processor

Clicking on the Command Line Processor icon opens a DOS window in which all of the DB2 environmental variables have been set.

## 5 • Tools

```
DB2 CLP - DB2.EXE
(c) Copyright IBM Corporation 1993,1995,1997
Command Line Processor for DB2 SDK 5.0.0

You can issue database manager commands and SQL statements from the command
prompt. For example:
       db2 => connect to sample
       db2 => bind sample.bnd

For general help, type: ?.
For command help, type: ? command, where command can be
the first few keywords of a database manager command. For example:
   ? CATALOG DATABASE for help on the CATALOG DATABASE command
   ? CATALOG         for help on all of the CATALOG commands.

To exit db2 interactive mode, type QUIT at the command prompt. Outside
interactive mode, all commands must be prefixed with 'db2'.
To list the current command option settings, type LIST COMMAND OPTIONS.

For more detailed help, refer to the Online Reference Manual.

db2 =>
```

The

```
db2 =>
```

prompt tells you that the DB2 command line processor has also been invoked. This simply means that you are in a position to type DB2 commands directly to DB2 and expect them to be carried out. So, for example, you can type

```
Connect to sample
Select * from org
```

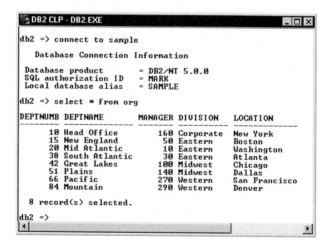

You can also try:

```
list node directory
```

Whether you get an intelligible reply or not will depend, in this case, not on the command line processor, but upon whether you understand what `list node directory` is asking for. In other words, the command line processor is mainly provided for the benefit of DB2 users who have experience in driving the earlier versions that do not have a GUI. Such people will find it invaluable, just as some Windows users resort to DOS on occasions. If you are new to DB2, our advice is that you will rarely need this feature.

However, the one thing you desperately need to know, having started it, is how to stop it. The crude way is simply to close the DOS window. More elegantly, from the

```
db2 =>
```

prompt you can type

```
terminate
```

which should return you to the DOS prompt, where you can type

```
exit
```

to close the window.

## Command Window

Clicking on the Command Window icon opens a DOS window in which all of the DB2 environmental variables have been set. In effect, you get a DOS prompt from which DOS users can issue their favorite DOS commands, like `dir`.

```
  DB2 CLP                                                          _ □ ×
07/02/97  08:53p           268,444 rexx.img
07/02/97  08:53p            73,728 rexxapi.dll
07/02/97  08:53p            99,328 rexxutil.dll
07/02/97  08:53p            26,624 rxapi.exe
06/27/97  09:17a             2,497 sqlar.dbg
06/27/97  09:17a             4,608 sqlar.dll
06/27/97  02:49p            17,408 strtstep.exe
            224 File(s)     43,974,801 bytes
                         1,044,949,504 bytes free

C:\SQLLIB\BIN>dir *.
 Volume in drive C has no label.
 Volume Serial Number is E400-D6C6

 Directory of C:\SQLLIB\BIN

07/18/97  03:35p        <DIR>          .
07/18/97  03:35p        <DIR>          ..
07/02/97  08:53p            20,554 asnmig
07/02/97  08:53p           300,318 asnmigh
07/02/97  08:53p           450,262 asnmigp
              5 File(s)       771,134 bytes
                         1,044,949,504 bytes free

C:\SQLLIB\BIN>exit
```

Once again, if DOS is not your bag, simply ignore this feature.

To close this window, just type 'exit'.

❥ *If you open up a Command Window and type:*

```
db2
```

*you essentially convert it to a Command Line Processor because the command 'db2' starts a copy of the Command Line Processor running. This rather nicely emphasizes the difference between these two: the Command Window is essentially a DOS window with environmental variables set. The Command Line Processor is essentially a DOS window with environmental variables set and the Command Line Processor running.* ❥

## The Big Eight

Eight of these tools form a natural group in that they are logically grouped together in DB2, and they can all be reached by using buttons on the Control Center toolbar.

The tools in question are:

- Control Center
- Command Center
- Script Center
- Alert Center
- Journal
- Tools Settings
- Event Analyzer
- Information Center

❥ *OK – so you noticed that we've listed eight tools and there are ten buttons. One of the extra buttons (third from the right) simply lists the legend for the graphics used in the Control Center:*

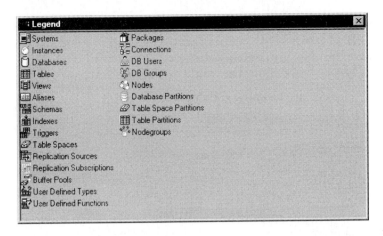

The other (extreme right) is a standard help button. Neither of these is a tool in the same sense that the others are tools. We haven't covered the rest of the buttons from left to right because we thought the order below made more sense. Hover help will tell you which button is which.

## Control Center

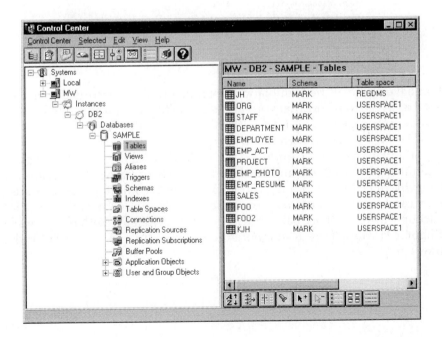

The Control Center you've already met, and it is the most important of all of the tools. It is from within the Control Center that you can create and manipulate the objects in databases, objects in this case being tables, views, users and so on. Once again we would encourage you to:

- Spend time getting to know the Control Center.
- Right-click on everything in sight, because right-clicking leads you to most of the functionality that the Control Center offers.

### Command Center

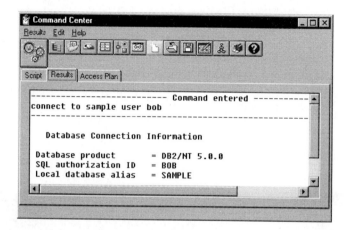

You have also met the Command Center before when testing the sample database. It is from here that you can type in DB2 commands and SQL commands. This makes it sound like the Command Line Processor, which is good because that's pretty much what it is – it's a GUI version of that tool.

The advantage of the Command Center lies in its ability to let you type in a number of commands and save them as a script (rather like creating a batch file of DOS commands). These scripts can become important because they can be used to automate processes in DB2 such as the all-important backup. However, since backup scripts can be generated with the GUI (see Chapter 11) our advice is to ignore the Command Center, at least for the time being.

## Script Center

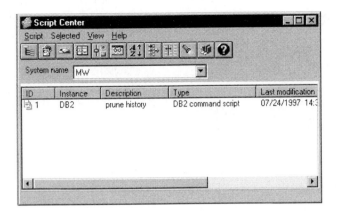

This tool lets you manipulate scripts. It also allows you to schedule scripts to run at particular times, run scripts immediately and generally maintain them.

In fact, when you create and save a script in the Command Center, it is automatically popped into the Script Center. You could be forgiven for wondering why we are making this point, having just advised you not to bother with the Command Center for now. True, we did, but scripts can come from other places. For example, when you use the backup Smart-Guide (see Chapter 11), that SmartGuide automatically generates a script for you. That script is also automatically sent to the Script Center. So, even if you never hand-craft a script, you are still very likely to need to manipulate scripts and the Script Center is the place where you will do it.

❝ *By the way – yes, the script is the screenshot really is called 'prune history'. We named this one after the DB2 command that it enacts. Better than that, it is actually a script that you might find useful (see Chapter 12 on Scheduling). Some dyed-in-the-wool DB2 users don't see the name as funny until it is pointed out to them. We avidly looked for 'Apricot Archives', 'Lemon Logs' and 'Mirabelle Myths' but sadly they aren't included in the DB2 command set.* ❞

When you decide to schedule a script to be run at a certain time, the script automatically appears in the Journal.

## Journal

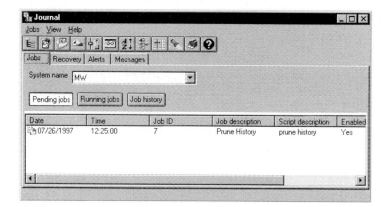

Once a script has been scheduled it is called a job, and all jobs appear in the Journal. Here you can see the jobs that are pending and those taking place at the moment. You can also inspect jobs that have already been completed and see the results – whether they were completed successfully or not. The DB2 Journal is a bit like a real-world journal; it's where you keep track of time-based events.

It's not just jobs that reside in the Journal, however. For example, if you click the Recovery tab and use the Select button to locate a particular database, you can see the options for recovering the database from a backup taken at a particular time. You can also use the Alerts tab to look at the alerts that DB2 has generated (more on these in Chapter 14) and finally the Messages tab to look at the warnings that DB2 issues. Despite the name, warnings are usually helpful rather than threatening.

## Alert Center

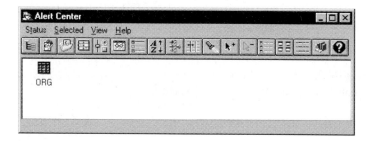

From the Alert Center you can see any alarms and warnings which have been generated by the Snapshot Monitor. If the Snapshot Monitor is set to issue a warning when a parameter reaches a certain level, that warning will appear in the Alert Center, giving you early notification of any potential problems. Colored icons represent different levels of warning, using the traffic light 'red – amber – green' color scheme.

## Tools Settings

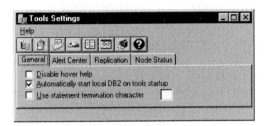

Tools Settings enables you to make general configuration changes to the other tools, such as whether you wish hover help turned off or on. Some of the settings are specific to one tool. So, for example, you can set the Alert Center to 'surface' (that is, to pop to the top layer of the screen) on new alarms and warnings (the default), on new warnings, or never.

## Event Analyzer

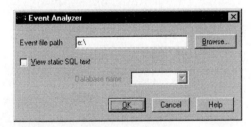

The Event Analyzer is used in conjunction with Event Monitoring (see above). An event monitor, as the name suggests, monitors events such as connections or transactions and compiles an event monitor file.

Using the Event Analyzer, the information contained in this file can be inspected.

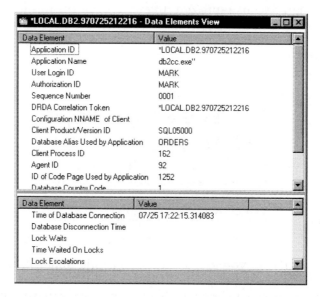

## Information Center

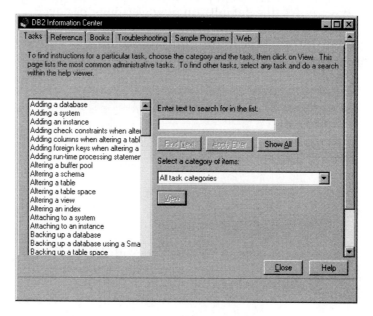

This gives you access to the comprehensive searchable on-line documentation for DB2, and you can also access the latest details from IBM's web sites.

Information is subdivided into areas like Tasks, Reference and Troubleshooting, among others. Hypertext links in the pages of help make it easy to navigate to the information you need.

## Summary

There are 19 tools here; too many to learn all at once. Which ones are you likely (realistically) to use extensively in the near future?

We think these are the most important when you are first getting to know DB2:

- Control Center
- Journal
- Alert Center
- Information Center
- Client Configuration Assistant (which we've covered in detail already)

By the time you have mastered these, you will have a good fundamental grasp of how the product works. In the next few chapters we'll be looking at specific tasks and you will find that these tools have a major part to play.

*Chapter 6*

# Creating Databases and Tables

Once upon a time, when the world was young, DB2 was used only to manage really large databases on serious mainframe hardware. Since the serious mainframes of that era were only about as powerful as a pocket calculator of today (OK, so it's an exaggeration, but you get the idea) the whole system often had to be tweaked as finely as possible before the performance was anywhere near acceptable.

Today the situation is different. For a start, DB2 is smarter than it used to be, so it can do a lot of the tuning for you (see Chapter 15). In addition, today's hardware is often powerful enough to cope with less than perfectly optimized databases.

So, whenever you create and use your first couple of databases, it is an excellent idea to accept the defaults and concentrate on learning the basics of DB2. However, as you work, you will find (if you dig around) that even the simple databases that you create with DB2 will have table spaces, containers, schemas and so on. These components are the very stuff of tuning, and even the simplest database has to have all of them in place before it can work.

Once you have become happy with creating and manipulating simple databases, it is worth getting to know about these components, even if only so that you can understand the default choices that are made. In addition, as you begin to create larger and more complex databases, you may well want to start changing the defaults.

Getting to grips with table spaces and containers is known to give people trouble at first. This is a shame for two reasons. One is that understanding them is only difficult in the sense that there is quite a lot of detail to absorb; the actual concepts are quite easy. Secondly, table spaces and containers can be really useful once your database grows to an appreciable size.

So, we'll run through the ideas behind table spaces and containers a couple of times, increasing the level of detail as we go. Hopefully this will keep the concepts clear as the detail is expanded.

# Containers and Table Spaces

## Overview

### Containers

In a database you want to store objects like tables, indexes and suchlike on disk. In a simplistic world you would store all of them in a single location on a single disk. For example, in the PC-based RDBMS called Access, all of the objects associated with a database are stored in a single file. That file is typically located in a subdirectory on the local drive.

This is fine in a PC-based RDBMS, but client–server systems can be more complex. For a start, you may want to assign different database objects to different areas of the file server's disk. Indeed, the file server may have multiple disks or other storage devices. These devices may have different performance characteristics (some may be faster than others), so you may want to assign different bits of the database to different devices. Typically, for example, performance is improved if indexes are placed on the fastest available drive.

These different areas where data can be stored are known as Containers in DB2. A container may be located on any device (though is typically a disk) that the server can use. A container can be an NT file, a subdirectory, or even an area of an unformatted hard disk.

### Table Spaces

In a complex database you might have, say, a hundred objects (such as tables) and ten containers. Each table has to be assigned to a container and, when the numbers grow to this sort of size, keeping track of which table is stored in which container can become a major pain.

In fact, we see almost exactly the same problem when managing users and resources on a network. Assigning rights to users on a network is rarely done on an individual basis. Instead users are grouped together in, well, groups, and rights are assigned to the group.

In the same way, if different tables were assigned to different containers on an individual basis, your workload would be very high. Enter (from stage left) the concept of table spaces. Table spaces are simply 'groups' for tables. You can allocate multiple tables to table spaces and allocate multiple containers to the table spaces.

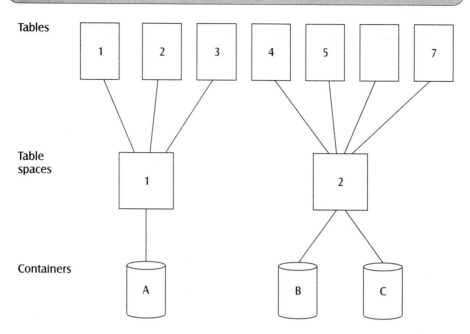

One absolute rule is that any given container is only ever allocated to a single table space.

One less than absolute rule is that each table is typically allocated to a single table space. This rule isn't absolute (hence it isn't really a rule), but to give you a feel for what you are likely to do on a day-to-day basis, tables are commonly allocated in this way. (We'll talk about some exceptions below.)

Looking at the diagram we can see that, for example, table 1 has been allocated to table space 1 and it is stored in container A. Table 2 is also allocated to the same table space and hence the same container.

Table 4 is in table space 2 and is located in containers B and C. Incidentally, this doesn't mean that table 2 is duplicated in containers B and C. It means that parts of table 2 are in container B and parts in container C. True, this means that if container C corrupts we lose table 4 (and in this case also tables 5, 6 and 7) but that's what we keep backups for. (You do keep backups, don't you?)

As you might imagine, there has to be an advantage in splitting tables across multiple containers, otherwise no one would bother. One is that data retrieval may be faster (see below); the second is that, as tables expand, you can add containers to the table space without disrupting the tables.

So far this all seems pretty simple (and it is!), but it is worth looking at a real example. During the installation of DB2 and SAMPLE on our Compaq, we accepted all of the defaults.

If we look at how the table spaces were assigned by DB2, it looks like this:

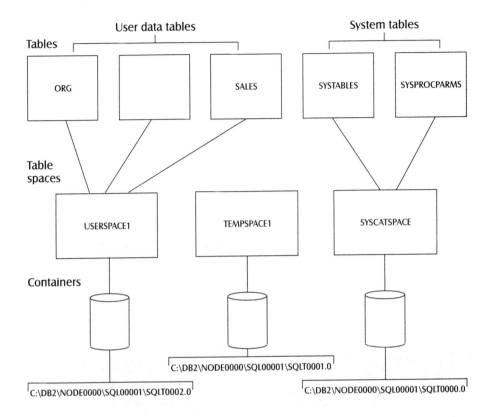

❝ *In practice there are nearly 40 system tables and nine user tables in the* SAMPLE *database; we just got bored after drawing the five that are shown on the diagram.* ❞

Note that in this case the 'containers' are subdirectories on the C: drive. Also note that there is a table space called TEMPSPACE1 which appears to be doing nothing; that is, no tables are associated with it. DB2 always creates a table space with this name by default. It is used to store 'scratch' tables – for example, the temporary tables that are produced during some SQL operations. The good news is that you don't have to worry too much about this table space since it usually looks after itself.

You can check to see if your installation is the same by using the Control Center. To see which table spaces are associated with the tables, open SAMPLE and select Tables and you should see the table spaces listed in the right-hand window.

# 6 • Creating Databases and Tables

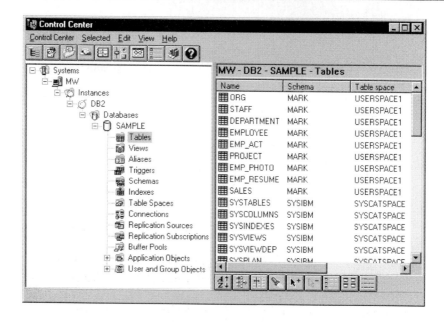

To check the allocation of containers to table spaces, select Table Spaces, right-click on, say, USERSPACE1 and select Alter.

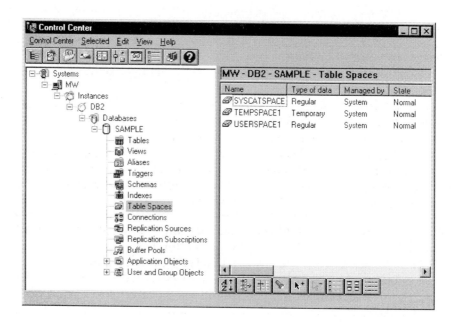

So, to summarize thus far, tables are allocated to table spaces and containers are allocated to table spaces. Each table space can have one or more containers, but each container can be allocated to only a single table space.

## More About Containers

Containers can be of three types:

- files
- subdirectories
- areas of a 'raw' unformatted disk

We'll have a look at them in more detail to see why there can be three types of container.

When you store data in a computer system, the 'normal' way to behave is to save it in a file that is managed by the operating system. Suppose, for example, that you use a word processor to write a letter and save it. You tell the word processor which folder and file name to use. In turn, the word processor passes that information to the OS, which looks after the messy business of writing the file to disk (where it might be written as hundreds of non-contiguous blocks).

Some RDBMSs work in the same way; they leave the mechanics of saving a table to disk to the operating system. The advantage of doing so is that it is easier (after all, that's what OSs are supposed to do). The disadvantage is that the access to the data in the table is slower because the OS has to be consulted about every read and write.

In order to speed things up, some RDBMSs (DB2 included) can also access disk space directly. The good news is that your database works faster; the bad news is that you need to put more effort into managing that disk space. For example, you have to estimate the size of tables when the container is created (although this isn't usually too taxing).

Effectively, therefore, DB2 can use two types of storage. There's the 'normal' storage (i.e. storage that is still managed by the OS), known as System Managed Space (SMS). There's also the faster type that is managed by the database: Database Managed Space (DMS).

|     | Size allocation | Speed |
| --- | --- | --- |
| SMS | Expands and contracts as the data changes size. Easy to manage. | Slow |
| DMS | Fixed size. You have to estimate the size of the table(s) when the container is created. | Fast |

So why are there three types of container (files, subdirectories, raw disk) if there are only two types of storage? Well, DMS can itself be composed of two types.

If you have an unformatted disk attached to your server, you can allocate all or part of this to be DMS. The fact that it is unformatted makes it inaccessible to the OS, but that doesn't matter because you use the database engine to manage it directly.

Now suppose that you don't have an unformatted disk but still want the benefits of DMS. What you can do is to get DB2 to create a file of fixed length (say, 50 Mbyte) which DB2 then manages. The OS knows that the file is there (and so the file appears in, for example, NT Explorer) but the OS doesn't manage the contents. Thus if the database puts 1 Mbyte of data in the file, that file will still occupy 50 Mbyte of disk space as far as the OS is concerned. This is the second kind of DMS and gives us the third type of container.

To summarize the types of container that you can have:

|     | Size allocation | Speed | Type |
| --- | --- | --- | --- |
| SMS | Expands and contracts as the data changes size. Easy to manage. | Slow | Subdirectory |
| DMS | Fixed size. You have to estimate the size of the table(s) when the container is created. | Fast | File |
| DMS | Fixed size. You have to estimate the size of the table(s) when the container is created. | Fast | Area of unformatted disk |

To provide a brief sanity check at this point, you can refer back to the installation of SAMPLE. There are three table spaces:

- SYSCATSPACE, which holds all of the system tables.
- TEMPSPACE1, which is a sort of 'scratch' space that is used during SQL operations for sorting or reorganizing tables.
- USERSPACE1, which stores all of the users' tables and objects, such as the indexes.

By default, each table space is assigned to its own container. On our Compaq these containers are subdirectories:

```
C:\DB2\NODE0000\SQL00001\SQLT0000.0
C:\DB2\NODE0000\SQL00001\SQLT0001.0
C:\DB2\NODE0000\SQL00001\SQLT0002.0
```

(your mileage may vary).

Since these containers are subdirectories, we can deduce that when the SAMPLE database was set up, these containers were created as SMS – System Managed Space.

## More About Table Spaces

Since the containers can be either SMS or DMS, it follows that table spaces can be classified in the same way. You are not allowed to allocate containers of both types to a single table space; therefore table spaces are either associated with SMS or with DMS containers, never both.

In addition to this classification, table spaces can also be classified in another way into three types:

- Regular
- Long
- Temporary

Regular table spaces store, well, regular sorts of data (much of the naming in DB2 is so logical it makes our job quite difficult!), so they will be the ones you use most commonly.

Long table spaces are specifically designed to store data from the 'long' data types LONG VARCHAR and LONG VARGRAPHIC. Both these data types are difficult to store efficiently because they can be so variable in length (up to 32 700 characters for LONG VARCHAR and up to 16 350 for LONG VARGRAPHIC). So, when you create a table space, you can define it to be for LONG data, whereupon it can hold these data types very efficiently.

To put this into perspective, if you create a table that includes a column of data type LONG VARCHAR and try to store it in a Regular table space, DB2 will allow you to do so. However, it is more efficient to store this sort of data in a Long table space. This is discussed in more detail below.

Temporary type table spaces, as has already been discussed, are used as a scratch area by DB2.

The interaction between the type of table space and the space management described above looks like this:

| Table space | SMS | DMS |
|---|---|---|
| Regular | Y | Y |
| Long |   | Y |
| Temporary | Y | Y |

(In other words, the only combination you can't have is a Long table space with its data managed by the OS.)

It is common for any given table to be associated with just one table space, but variations are not too exceptional. For example, for performance reasons you might want to store the data from a table in one table space, and the indexes associated with that table in another table space. In that sense, the table would be associated with two table spaces.

The indexes are normally stored in the table space associated with the faster device. In fact, when indexes are assigned specifically to their own table space(s), these have to be DMS table space(s).

Now suppose that you had a table in which some of the columns were of type LONG VARCHAR or LONG VARGRAPHIC. You could store the entire table in a Long table space, but an alternative is to store the bulk of the columns in a Regular table space and only store the data from the LONG data types in a Long table space.

Finally, you can mix and match these, so that a table can actually be stored in three table spaces – a Regular one for the regular data, a Long one for the LONG data and a third for the indexes (which would be of type Regular).

The only thing that you have to watch is that, if you *do* assign indexes and/or long columns to separate table spaces then the primary table space (the one into which the rest of the data from the table is going) has to be a DMS rather than an SMS.

In case it isn't obvious why the statement in the last paragraph is true, a brief recap may help. As stated earlier, DB2 will allow you to assign more than one table space to a table. However, all table spaces allocated to a table must either be SMS or DMS, not a mixture of both. In the case mentioned above, if long data and indexes are assigned to separate table spaces, those must be DMS table spaces (DB2 won't allow anything else). So the primary table space would also have to be DMS.

Phew! We've finished the classification – no more to come!

## Summary so Far

You don't have to read this bit, but it might be helpful if all of the information above was new to you.

- Tables are allocated to table spaces.
- One table can be allocated to one or more table spaces.
- One table space can have one or more tables allocated to it.
- Containers are allocated to table spaces.
- One container can be allocated to one and only one table space.
- One table space can have one or more containers allocated to it.
- Table spaces can be 'typed' or classified as follows:

Table spaces can be:
- DMS
- SMS

Table spaces can be:
- Regular
- Long
- Temp

These two classifications interact as follows:

| Table space | SMS | DMS |
|---|---|---|
| Regular | Y | Y |
| Long |  | Y |
| Temporary | Y | Y |

- Containers can be 'typed' or classified as follows:

Containers can be:
- DMS
- SMS

Containers can be:
- Subdirectories
- Files
- Raw, unformatted disk space

These two classifications interact as follows:

| Containers | Management |
|---|---|
| Subdirectories | SMS |
| Files | DMS |
| Raw | DMS |

- Long data types *can* be stored in SMS. However, this type of data is more efficiently stored in a Long table space, which must be DMS and hence must use a DMS container.
- Indexes can be stored in SMS. They can also be stored in separate table spaces. If so, those table spaces must be DMS.
- Tables can make use of multiple table spaces, but those table spaces must be of the same type – either all SMS or all DMS.

## Why You Want to Know All of This

Table spaces and containers are not really conceptually difficult at all, but as you can see they provide a bean counter's paradise. It seems that each object type (table, table space and container) can be not only classified, but some can be classified in several different ways.

Very few people actually enjoy this sort of thing unless it can be shown to bring some benefit. Happily, there is advantage to be gained from understanding this process. We could list them all, but running over a few examples may help to give the idea better.

❢ *We are about to use the term 'small' in reference to a database. Clearly this can mean all sorts of different things to different people. We have genuinely dealt with people who said 'It's a really big database, well over a Mbyte'. At the other end of the scale, we know of several databases that are pushing 5 terabytes.*

*As far as this discussion goes, a small database is one that, given your usual number of users, doesn't stretch your hardware particularly. A large database is one that does. It's simple, really.*

*Oh, and a medium-sized database is sort of part-way between a small one and a large one. We know it's a bit vague, but never mind.* ❥

If you were creating a small database then our advice would be to forget about table spaces and containers. If you use the SmartGuides to create the database and tables, then it will allocate default names and use SMS. Easy.

If your database is larger and you want to use Long data types efficiently, you will have to set up two DMS table spaces, one for the regular data and one for the Long data. In turn, this means that you need at least two DMS containers. Assuming that you don't have extra disks attached to your server, the most likely option is that you will set up the containers as subdirectories on drive C:. The only tricky bit is that you will need to guess how large the containers have to be at the time you set them up.

If your database is heavily indexed, you may want to allocate the indexes to a separate table space that uses a container on a different disk. Again, the container and the table space will have to be DMS.

This brings us to one of the main reasons why table spaces and containers are so useful. Imagine a medium-sized database. This database is composed of many tables that have a multiplicity of joins between them. Image that the data is frequently queried and that the queries usually span many tables. Finally, imagine that the data is often updated. All of these factors mean that the indexes will be frequently read (by the queries) and updated (by the updates). If the indexes are stored on the same disk as the data, the reads from, and writes to, the indexes may become so frequent that they interfere with the access to the actual data. By separating the indexes and the data on separate disks you can remove the bottleneck. In fact it is usual in these cases to put the indexes on the faster device since index access is often more limiting than data access.

You can get the same sort of effect (that is, a faster database) by assigning multiple containers to the same table space. DB2 will balance the data across the different containers and, assuming that the containers are located on different devices, you may well see a speed gain.

Clearly this form of optimization is a complex subject. We haven't covered anything like all of the possibilities, we just want to show you *why* it is worth getting to know about table spaces and containers. The benefit they bring is a very high degree of flexibility in that they allow you to configure and fine tune the database for optimal performance.

OK, let's put this theory into practice.

## Creating a Database

We'll start with the assumption that you have already used the Smart-Guide to create a small, default database. Now you want to go to the next stage. The database you want to create will still be small, but more complex because you want to try out the options discussed above.

On our system we have two disks to hand, C: and E:. We are going use both of them, and we are going to use DMS to store the user tables and the catalog tables. We're going to store the temporary tables in SMS. So we'll create two subdirectories (using Explorer) called:

- C:\Penguin
- E:\Penguin

into which the database can go.

We are going to describe the choices we make, but you can specify different drives, subdirectory and file names as you see fit.

Having created those, from the Control Center right-click on **Databases** and select **Create, New**

## 6 • Creating Databases and Tables

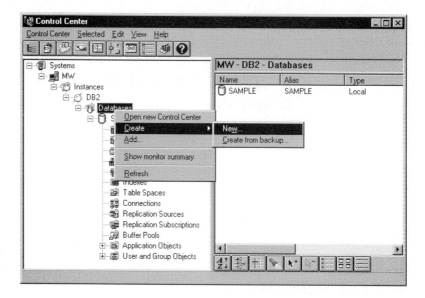

and the Create Database SmartGuide will start up. In page 1 give the database a name (we'll use `TEST`) and leave the default drive set to C:.

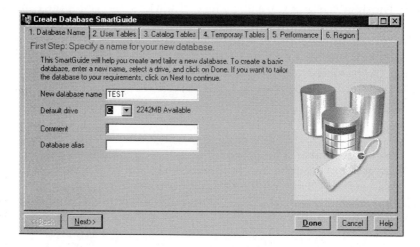

In page 2, choose High performance, and use the Add button to create a 100 Mbyte file called `UserTbls` in `C:\Penguin`.

To provide a reality check at this point, what you are creating at this point is a container. This container is DMS (because you chose High performance) and it is a file (called `C:\Penguin\UserTbls`). This container will be used for the user tables that you create in the database. Incidentally,

## 6 • Creating Databases and Tables

the text on the pages of the SmartGuide is well worth reading as you go through this exercise.

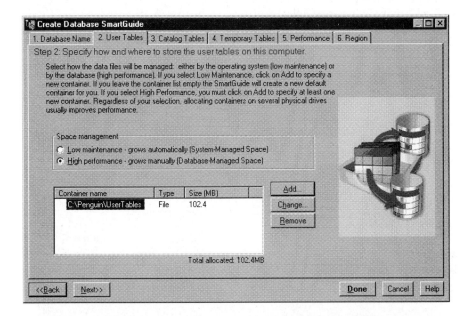

The next page lets you create a container for the catalog tables. We'll elect to store these in C:\Penguin as a 50 Mbyte file called CatTbls.

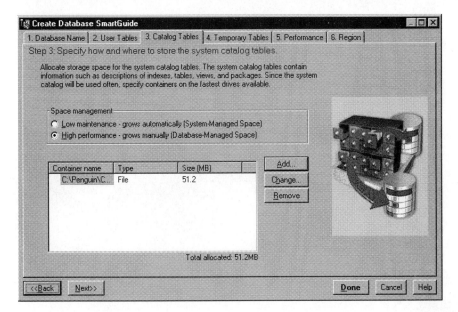

Finally, to provide variation, we are going to store the temporary tables in SMS on drive E: in \Penguin2. (We aren't suggesting this is an optimal strategy, but it lets you see the different options that are possible.) In page 4 select Low maintenance, click on the Add button, navigate to drive E: and type in the name for the new subdirectory (note that we didn't create this one before starting).

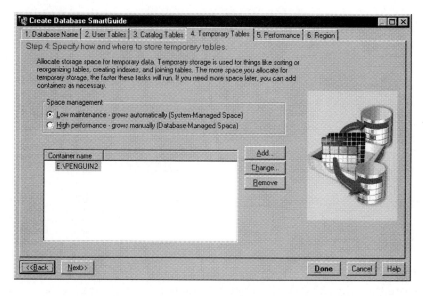

Page 5

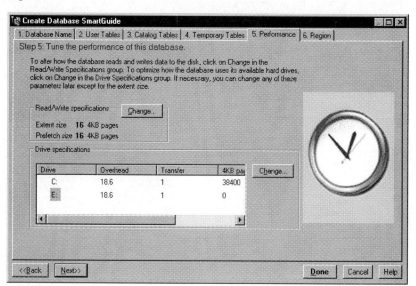

# 6 • Creating Databases and Tables

asks (if you click on the Change button) about the size of tables and the number of containers in each table space.

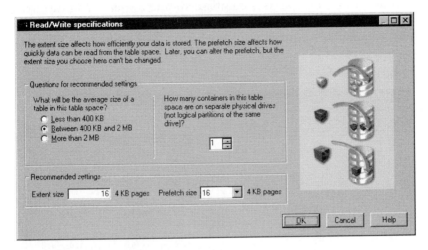

Given this information, DB2 will configure two parameters: the extent size and the prefetch size. (You can safely ignore these parameters for the moment and, if you feel moved to do so, investigate at your leisure.) The defaults are reasonable for now, but we recommend that you have a look at the questions DB2 asks here because you may want to provide this information in a production database.

Page 6 is interesting:

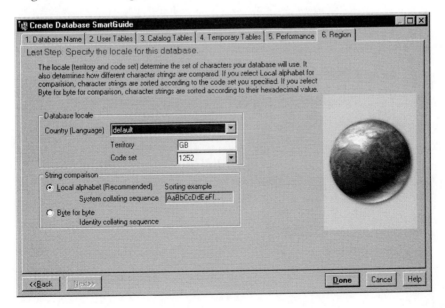

but again you should probably accept the defaults and then press Done.

DB2 should whirr and buzz for a while (a dialog appears with cogs whirling around) and then the new database should appear. You can inspect your new creation using the Control Center; you should find a raft of catalog tables (if no tables appear, you may have a filter operating), but no user tables as yet.

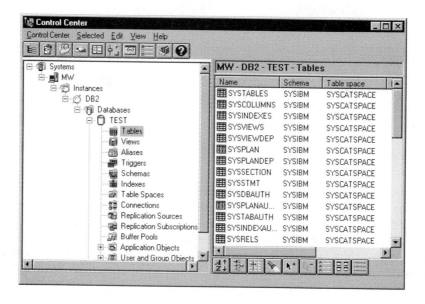

You should find three table spaces (try scrolling in the right-hand window, where there is more information about each).

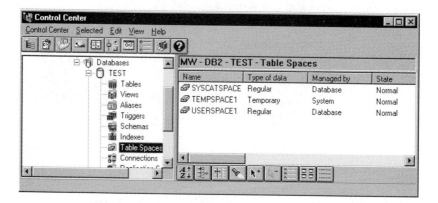

The SmartGuide automatically generated these table spaces. If you double click one of them you can find out more about it, and sure enough there is one of the containers you specified.

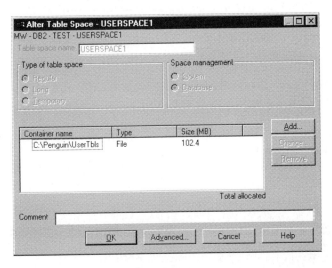

If you want to create a table now, you can use the SmartGuide as before, and hopefully the options on page 5 will mean more to you than when we ran through it in Chapter 2.

Rather than demonstrate the SmartGuide again, we'll use the dialog box to create a table. In the Control Center, right-click on Tables and choose Create, Table.

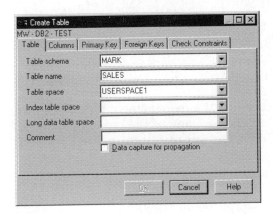

On the first page, just select a name and USERSPACE1 as the table space. On the remaining pages you can add columns, set a primary key etc. This is very much like the SmartGuide without the glitz and shouldn't present too many problems. If you choose VARCHAR as a data type, DB2 will let you do so (whether you can choose VARGRAPHIC or LONG VARGRAPHIC will depend upon how DB2 is set up, so you may want to avoid these for the present). However, if you go back to page 1 and try to specify a different table space for the Long data, nothing appears in the pop-down list. Why not?

The answer is that we have three containers (two are DMS and one is SMS). We also have three table spaces (two are DMS and one SMS). However, none of the table spaces is for Long data. No problem; we'll create one.

From the Control Center right-click on Table Spaces and select Create, Table space using Smart Guide.

In page 1 enter a table space name (we chose LongData), in page 2 select Long.

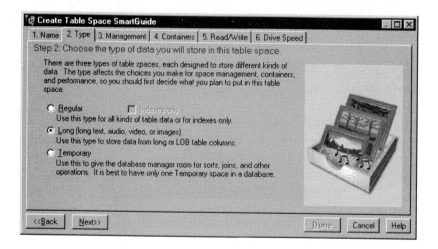

In page 3 you choose the management type (SMS or DMS), but given that you have just chosen Long as the type of data, you'll find that high performance (DMS) has already been selected for you (and you can't change it).

## 6 • Creating Databases and Tables

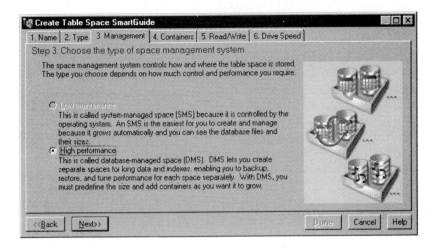

Next (page 4) you choose the containers. You can't choose any of the ones you have already defined (each container can only be allocated to one table space) so you define a new one. We'll define a 200 Mbyte file called `E:\Penguin\LongData`.

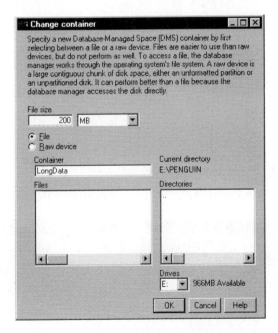

Pages 5 and 6 ask for information that will depend upon your database and server. When you have looked at them and made your choices, press Done.

The new table space appears in the database.

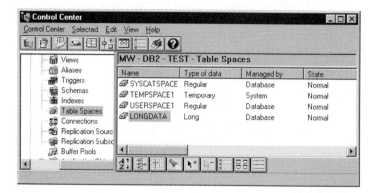

Now if you create another table, you can allocate a separate table space for the Long data

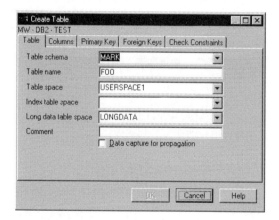

and the Control Center will show both table spaces being used.

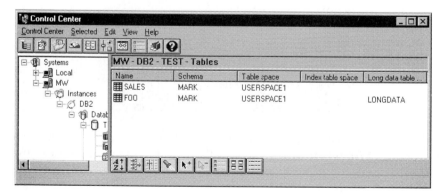

So we have shown you how to create containers for the default table spaces, and how to create new table spaces with new containers. The only important bit remaining is the process of adding a container to an existing table space. You would do this either because the existing table space was nearly full, or in order to improve performance.

Using two containers on different devices for the same table space usually improves performance. This will, of course, depend on the speed and location of the devices in question.

This is really easy. Simply double click on the table space, click the Add button in the dialog box that appears and add a new container.

The only areas of table design that we haven't covered here are Primary and Foreign keys, and they are covered in the next chapter which is about integrity.

## Summary

In this chapter we have covered the background to table spaces, containers and so on, and have shown you the various steps you can take to make use of them. We haven't shown you how to build a fully optimized database using these principles and techniques because the steps you will take depend on your available hardware and the database you are creating.

In addition, as we have said before, there is much more detail in the manuals, and now that you (hopefully) have a good grounding in the subject, you will be able to understand and make use of the comprehensive information in IBM's documentation.

*Chapter 7*

# Integrity and Indexes

The bad news is that if people enter data into your database you cannot guarantee that the data is error-free. People make mistakes, and not all are detectable (at least not by the database). The good news is that several classes of error *are* detectable and therefore preventable. For example, if you keep a list of existing customers in a CUSTOMER table, you can ensure that the customer's name is always spelled consistently no matter where it appears in the database.

There are several tools/schemes/systems which are designed to reduce the errors that are introduced into your data by detectable errors, thus increasing (and/or protecting) the integrity of your data; numbered among these tools are Constraints. These allow, as the name suggests, constraints to be placed on the values which are acceptable in certain columns.

## Primary Constraints (Referential Integrity)

Primary and foreign keys are your first and most vital lines of defense against inaccurate data (sometimes delightfully known as 'dirty data'), since they allow you to enforce referential integrity. This form of integrity protection is common to all RDBMS, and DB2 enforces it in the normal way. We suspect that most of you will understand the theory behind referential integrity since it is so commonly employed, and we aren't going to discuss it in detail. However, if you feel the need to know more about the theory behind it, please consult the book mentioned in the Introduction, which covers this topic in some depth.

What we will do is to show you how to implement these keys in DB2.

## Adding Primary and Foreign Keys to Tables

We'll look at building a couple of tables with primary and foreign keys. Since you've already seen the table-building SmartGuide, this time we'll use the dialogs to create the tables.

For our example we'll create two tables. One (CUSTOMER) will contain customer records and each customer will have a unique identifier. The other (ORDER) will hold records of orders placed by these customers. Each record in the ORDER table will have its own unique identifier; in addition, it will carry a reference to the customer who placed it. This reference will act as the foreign key to the primary key in the CUSTOMER table.

We're assuming you have a database in which to work; we'll use the existing TEST database, first having cleaned out all the tables that we created earlier. Table spaces and containers have been defined for this database, and we'll just allow DB2 to assign the defaults because we want to concentrate on the key definitions here.

From the Control Center, click to expand the TEST database object, right-click on Tables and choose Create, Table (not Create, Table using SmartGuide).

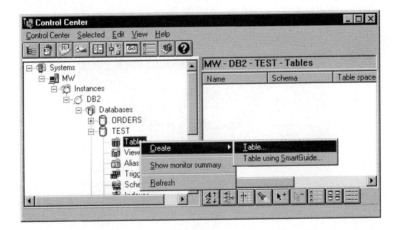

## 7 • Integrity and Indexes

On the Table page of the dialog, fill in a name for the table; ours is CUSTOMER – uninspired but workable. You can ignore the rest of this page – though if you want to practice setting table spaces, go ahead.

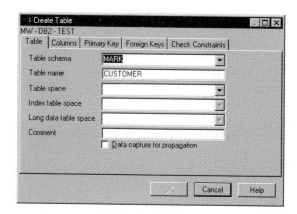

On the Columns page, click the Select button and you can choose columns from lists, just as you can in the SmartGuide. We've taken the first four from the Customers list, including CUSTOMER_ID. Click OK.

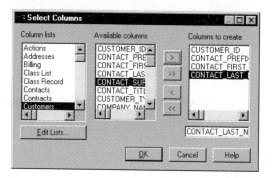

CUSTOMER_ID is to be our primary key, and as such must not be allowed to contain null values. Highlight that column and click on the Nullable check box to remove the check mark so that nulls cannot be entered into the column (as shown in the next screenshot).

# 7 • Integrity and Indexes

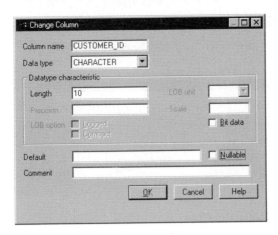

In the primary key page, the first column, CUSTOMER_ID, is already highlighted. Click the arrowhead button to shift it over into the primary key list.

❻ *The constraint name will become the name of the index that is associated with the primary key. You don't have to supply a name here, and if you don't, DB2 will generate an unwieldy one for you. A memorable name of your own choosing is a much better option.*

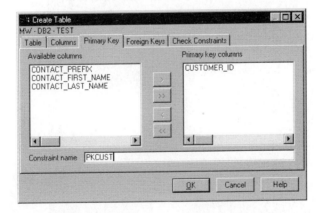

There are no foreign keys or check constraints in this table, so click on OK to finish the table creation process.

Now do the same again to create a table called ORDER. We selected the first five columns from the Order list after checking that CUSTOMER_ID was among them. ORDER_ID will be the primary key for this table, so set it to be Not Nullable.

## 7 • Integrity and Indexes

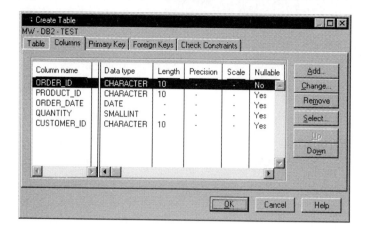

Define ORDER_ID as the primary key.

In the Foreign key dialog, the top part is concerned with the parent table. This will be the CUSTOMER table, so select it from the pop down list for Table Name. Its primary key is identified for you and shown to the right.

In the lower part of the page, the available columns in the ORDER table are shown on the left. Select CUSTOMER_ID to be the foreign key to the CUSTOMER_ID primary key in the parent table CUSTOMER.

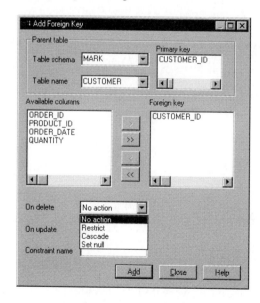

Various actions can be associated with delete and update events; for example, Cascade Delete can be set from here. (Some of these actions are specific to DB2, and a quick press of the F1 key reveals what they mean.)

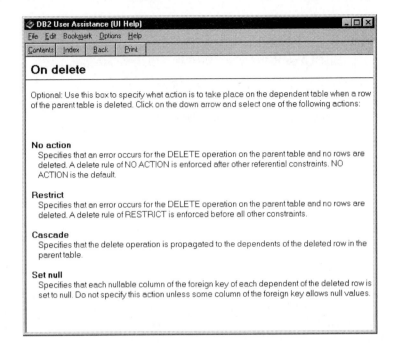

We feel that an obvious omission from this list is cascade update. Why this isn't available as an option is a mystery, known only to IBM.

Make your selection (we've elected to set Cascade Delete) and add a constraint name.

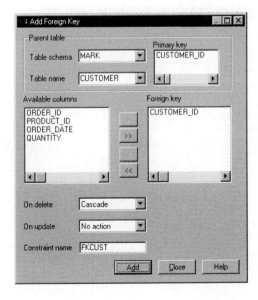

Then click on Add to add the foreign key. Finally close this dialog box

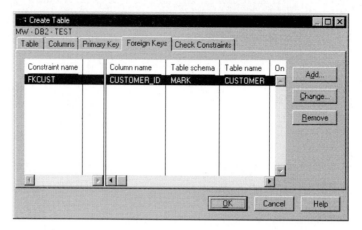

and click on OK to complete the creation of the ORDER table.

If you now go to the Indexes section of the object tree in the Control Center, you can see evidence of the two primary keys we created. If you gained experience with a product like Access, this may come as a surprise. In DB2, declaring a column (or columns) to be a primary key automatically generates an explicit index which exists as an object within the database. Out of interest (and only if you are drawn to do so) you can double click on either of these to see how it is structured.

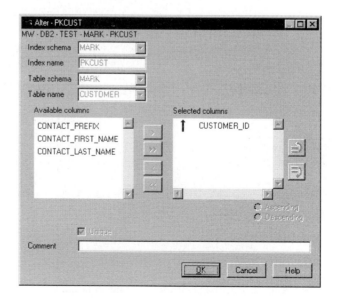

Now you can use your favorite front-end to connect to the database and start entering data into the tables. Here we have entered three customer records and are in the process of entering some orders. The first one is fine, but the second, which has a value of 9 in the CUSTOMER_ID field, cannot be inserted into the table because there is no customer with an ID of 9.

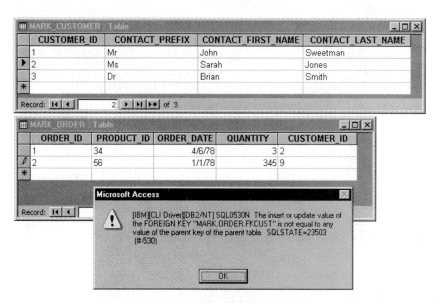

In the next case, some more records have been added to the ORDER table, and we are about to delete customer 2 from the CUSTOMER table.

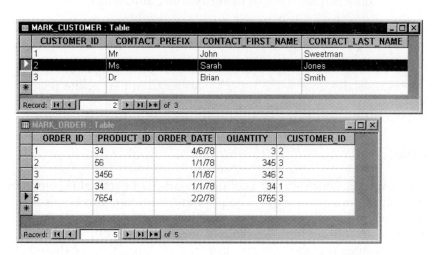

After the record has been deleted and after we refresh the view in Access, we can see that the associated records in the CUSTOMER table have also been deleted.

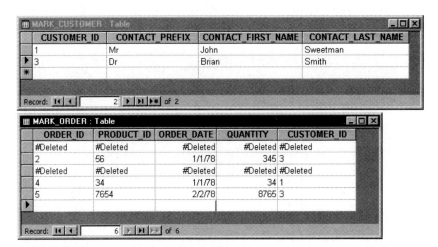

This is because we set Cascade Delete as an option during the definition of the foreign key.

## Other Types of Integrity Constraint

DB2 offers three further types of integrity constraint, which are:

- Unique
- NOT NULL (already touched upon)
- Check constraints

Of these, only the third is DB2-specific rather than part of the relational model itself (certainly in implementation), so we'll look at it in more detail than the others.

### Unique

Placing a unique constraint on a column means that each value contained in the column must be unique. Unique constraints can also be placed on multiple columns.

Suppose you store information about students in a STUDENT table and about the courses that they can take in a COURSE table. You can then create an ATTEND table which records which student attends which course.

# 7 • Integrity and Indexes

| StudentID | CourseID |
|---|---|
| 34 | 16 |
| 34 | 23 |
| 45 | 16 |
| 45 | 27 |
| 45 | 34 |

Clearly, in this table, a particular value for StudentID can appear multiple times, as can a given value for CourseID. However, we might well want to forbid two entries like this:

| StudentID | CourseID |
|---|---|
| 34 | 16 |
| 34 | 16 |

which implies that a student is attending the same course twice.

In DB2, if you want to place a unique constraint on a particular column or columns, you have to index that/those column(s).

❛ *Incidentally, this is why we talk about integrity and indexes in the same chapter (just in case you though we had put them together because they both start with 'I'). So we'll leave a description of how you actually set up a unique constraint until we've talked about setting up an index.* ❜

The reason DB2 insists that unique constraints are only applied to indexed columns is self-evident as soon as you imagine what would happen if this restriction *wasn't* applied. If DB2 allowed a unique constraint to be applied to an unindexed column, then every row would have to be examined (to ensure that the incoming one was unique) before an entry could be added or updated. Given a table with ten million rows this could become a little tedious.

A unique constraint in DB2 is automatically enforced on the columns that are declared to be primary keys.

## NOT NULL

The NOT NULL constraint, not unreasonably, prevents null values being entered into a column and is enforced simply by unchecking the Nullable option when adding columns during the process of creating a table. This can be done for any column, but *must* be done for columns that are destined to be primary keys (as described above).

## Check Constraints

The third type of constraint is a check constraint. Its role is to check that any value entered into a column adheres to the conditions defined in the check constraint. This check constraint can work within a column (the value entered in column X must be between 100 and 1000) and also between columns (the value in column X must be greater than the value in column Y). Check constraints are one of the most important tools for enforcing business rules.

Suppose your organization is based in a building that is divided into zones, and each zone is identified by a color. There are three color zones (Purple, Blue and Silver) and every staff member's room is in one of these zones. In the staff table, there is a column for the room number and another for the zone. You can add a check constraint to ensure that the value is 'Purple', 'Blue' or 'Silver' and never anything else (like 'Pinky-russet' or other flights of artistic interpretation).

Check constraint conditions are defined using the usual operators; the example above would look like this:

```
ZONE IN ('Purple', 'Blue', 'Silver')
```

Another example is:

```
DEPTNUMB BETWEEN 4500 AND 9000
```

Clearly each of these check constraints is working within a single column. However, a check constraint such as:

```
STARTDATE > BIRTHDATE
```

is constraining data between two columns and is considerable more powerful.

It must be possible to evaluate the condition of a check constraint by inspecting a single row of the table to which the check constraint is attached. The example above which checks that the date on which an employee started work is later than his or her date of birth is permissible so long as the two fields, STARTDATE and BIRTHDATE, are in the same table. If, for whatever bizarre reason, a separate table of birth dates was kept, that particular rule would not be enforceable with a check constraint. (It is still enforceable, but you would have to use a trigger to do it – these are covered in Chapter 13.)

Check constraints are evaluated every time an insert or update operation is performed. The restriction of the scope of a check constraint to within a single table has the benefit that each check constraint can be evaluated very rapidly. If the value in question does not conform to the rules, the transaction fails, the operation is rolled back and the field (or fields) remain unchanged. (See Chapter 11 for definitions of these terms.)

Each table can have multiple check constraints, and each check constraint can work on one or more columns, such as:

```
STAFFID <5000 AND DIVISION IN ('Eastern',
'Western', 'Corporate', 'Midwest')
```

For ease of identification, each check constraint can be named.

Creating check constraints is mind-numbingly easy. Assuming you have an existing table to which you intend to add them, double click on the table name in the Control Center and choose the Check Constraints tab.

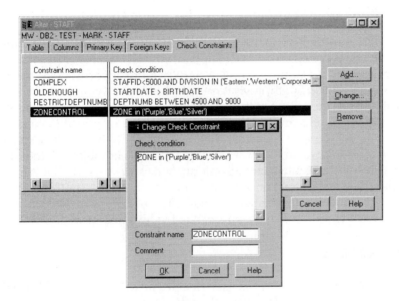

Here we are applying the constraints described to a STAFF table. In the next screenshot we have entered a row into the table.

As you can see, the data conforms to the constraints above.

Any attempt to violate those constraints was met with opposition.

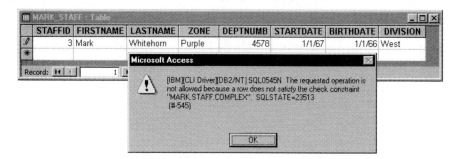

# Indexes

Indexes are a further component of DB2 and are used to speed access to the data. Why do we need them? Well, suppose you have a table of customers that has a customer ID column and a LASTNAME column. If you ask DB2 to find all the customers called Smith, it will have to look at every record in order to work out if it contains the name Smith. 'Ah', you suggest, 'why not sort the records so that all of the Smiths are together?'. Apart from the overhead in continually moving them around, if they are sorted by LASTNAME they can't be sorted by any other column, so any searches on those will be painfully slow. Indexes are essentially lists that contain enough information to allow DB2 to find rows very rapidly. They can be based on a single column (such as LASTNAME) or on multiple columns. Indexes are created automatically whenever you define a primary key field in a table; it is also possible to build indexes manually.

## Using Indexes

Once an index is in place, DB2 itself decides how it can best optimize performance using information from the tables themselves and from indexes. You don't *have* to deal with indexes at all; they're created automatically on essential columns and are used automatically by the system. You need only become involved when a need is perceived for further performance gains that might be achievable using indexes.

## Why Index?

Indexes add speed, a precious commodity for anyone with a database system to manage. Using indexes can give a considerable increase in the performance of queries, especially those that search for a particular value or range of values in a column.

An index is also able to order the rows in a table; it doesn't actually move the rows around so that they sit in order in the table but uses pointers to give the same effect. An ascending index on a CITY field knows that Toronto comes before Vancouver, even if Toronto occupies the last row in the table. This ability to order rows helps speed the processing of GROUP BY and ORDER BY queries if you are grouping and ordering on an indexed field.

The downside is that indexes impose overheads on a system. Each index must be maintained; every time a value is added or altered in an indexed field, indexes are also updated to reflect the change. Each index also takes up some storage space on disk. Despite these overheads, a set of carefully designed indexes can bring huge overall performance gains.

## What Should be Indexed?

So, with DB2 taking care of indexing primary key fields automatically, which others, if any, should you index? This depends on your data and the use made of it. As with other aspects of designing a database system, the final decisions can only be made by someone with an intimate knowledge of the data and the ways in which it will be used.

Having applied that rider, think seriously about indexing foreign key fields. Queries often find data via foreign keys ('Show me the total value of all orders taken by each of my employees') and indexing such columns can produce huge speed gains.

As a more general rule, indexes should be applied to the columns in each table that are used most frequently to locate data. If your users constantly identify orders by the buyer's surname rather than by the unique order code number, then adding an index on the surname is likely to be beneficial. Or, if many of the queries run against a database are based on delivery dates, an index on that field could be helpful.

If a table is updated frequently, you should be aware that creating a large number of indexes for it might slow access speeds.

Optimizing indexes is more of an art than a science, and there's no substitute for experience and experimentation. It's good to know that indexes are easily dropped if they don't bring the hoped-for gains. (DB2's use of the verb 'to drop' is somewhat drastic; a dropped object ceases to exist, vanishing permanently from the system.)

## Creating an Index

To create an index, in the Control Center right-click on the Indexes and select Create. In the Create Index window, specify the schema and name for the new index, and the schema and name for the table to which the index is to be added.

Under Available columns, highlight a column to be indexed and click the right arrow button to move it into the Selected columns list. Add further columns if necessary – the order in which they sit in the Selected columns list is the order in which the index is created. The column or columns selected comprise the index key.

If you want to specify that the column(s) must not contain duplicate values for the index key, click on the Unique check box. If duplicate values are already present in the table, the index is not created.

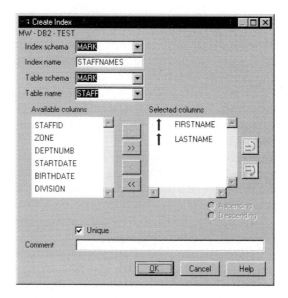

In this screenshot we are specifying that staff members can only ever have unique names. Thus we cannot have, for example, more than one Mark Whitehorn. We are not suggesting that this is a sensible restriction; it simply illustrates how indexes can be used.

*Part 2*

# Finer Control of Your Database

*Chapter 8*

# Users, Authorities and Privileges

We said in Chapter 1 that you had to install DB2 from a user account with NT administrator privileges and a username with eight or fewer characters. That user automatically acquired SYSADM authority and we suggested that you continue to use that account while following the examples.

We suggested this because the book isn't aimed at people who will be simply entering or querying the data. It is aimed at people who will be installing, setting up, running, maintaining and generally playing about with DB2, and they need power. *You* need power to administer an RDBMS, but too much power in the wrong hands can be dangerous, or at least undesirable.

Towards this end, DB2 provides a raft of ways of controlling access to both the workings of DB2 and to the data. This control is accomplished with a system of authorities and privileges that are allocated to users and groups of users. Essentially, authorities and privileges give you control over who is allowed to do what, and the system is almost infinitely flexible. Happily, to get a system under way there are four predefined levels of authority at which we will look after a brief foray into the subject of users and groups.

## Users and Groups

Any individual who accesses a database can be described as a user, and there can be anywhere between one and thousands of users on a system. When you reach the stage of having thousands of anything, some means of dealing with them other than individually is called for, so in client–server systems a collection of users can be declared to be a group. The users in a group can be described as its membership. All users of DB2 have automatic membership of the predefined group called PUBLIC.

Groups often map neatly to the jobs that people do, for instance, into such divisions as programming, management and sales. It is usually true that people who do the same job require the same sorts of tools to work with, so treating them as a group makes a lot of sense, and that in turn makes a great deal of sense when determining the privileges that users should be given.

One of the great advantages of groups is that they make the allocation of privileges very easy. Instead of allocating them to individuals it is common practice to allocate privileges to groups, whereupon each member of that group acquires those privileges. Rather than implementing its own grouping mechanism, DB2 very sensibly makes use of NT's groups. We'll talk about how this works in practice below.

## Authorities

An authority allows any user who holds it to carry out certain administrative functions, and is typically assigned to groups of users rather than to individuals.

There are four authorities:

- SYSADM – System Administration Authority
- SYSCTRL – System Control Authority
- SYSMAINT – System Maintenance Authority
- DBADM – Database Administrator Authority

❢ *Now seems like a good time to say again that these four terms are DB2-specific. We purposely use a non-DB2-specific acronym (DBA) in this book to refer to a general person (like you) who is interested in controlling a database. When you actually run a production DB2 system you might be a SYSADM or a DBADM (or SYSADM on one system and SYSMAINT on another). We only use the DB2 terms when we mean them specifically; otherwise we'll use the more generic DBA.* ❣

Three of these authorities are instance-level authorities; that is, they give control over an entire DB2 instance, regardless of how many databases may be running therein. The only one that isn't instance-level (and is therefore database-level) is DBADM.

We'll run through what these authorities mean, and who should have them. However, bear in mind that there is no obligation upon you to grant these authorities just because they exist. Their role in life is to make the day-to-day running and maintenance of a system easier, and if they just add a layer of complexity then they aren't really doing their job. Use the ones you need; if it's just one SYSADM, or maybe a SYSADM and a couple of DBADMS, then that's fine. Use the flexibility to suit you and your organization.

## SYSADM

SYSADM has the highest level of authority available. As the installer of DB2 you automatically acquired this authority – you are all-seeing and all-powerful. So, SYSADM is top dog, and depending on the size of the system you may be the sole top dog or be one of a pack (sorry, group). In many organizations it makes sense to have several SYSADMs to provide redundancy for illness, holidays and unforeseen emergencies such as an attack of megalomania.

What can you do with all this power? *Everything*. As SYSADM you have all the privileges going and can issue any DB2 command and expect to have it fulfilled. You can access the data in any database in an instance and have control over all the objects in an instance (tables, views, indexes, table spaces, aliases – the lot).

You can also grant authorities and privileges to others. If you think of a branching tree-like structure (though with the tree turned upside-down, which rather makes a mockery of the analogy) SYSADM is right at the top; below it sit all other authorities and below them the users and groups with various types of privilege.

The ability to grant and revoke authorities and privileges to others is an important part of the whole system. As a general rule, you can never grant a higher authority than the one you hold yourself, and you cannot even grant the authority you hold to another. SYSADM is the exception; but then we knew that, because SYSADM can do anything.

## SYSCTRL

Only a SYSADM can grant the SYSCTRL level of authority. SYSCTRL has full system control authority, with all of the power necessary to manage the system – just like SYSADM. So, how do the two differ? The only difference is that SYSCTRL doesn't have the ability to read and modify the data, which is an interesting distinction. SYSCTRL is able to maintain an instance and its databases, having the authority to create and drop databases, to create, drop or alter table spaces and even to force users off the system – but he or she just can't look at the data in the tables.

There is nothing to stop a SYSADM deciding to give data read and/or modify privileges to a SYSCTRL (say, for a particular table); that's the benefit of high configurability.

❝ *We suspect that organizations like the FBI and CIA just love this feature and for some systems it makes perfect sense to divorce the power to manage the system from the ability to read all of the data. After all, though it pains us to admit it, computer people are not inherently any more trustworthy than anyone else. Having said that, for many systems this type of paranoia is unnecessary and SYSCTRL won't be required.* ❞

### SYSMAINT

Again, System Maintenance authority can only be granted by SYSADM. SYSMAINT is a lower level of system control authority than SYSCTRL, having a subset of its powers. A SYSMAINT can perform tasks like backing up a database or table space, restoring an existing database, carrying out roll forward recovery (see Chapter 11) and starting or stopping a database instance. In other words, as the name suggests, this level of authority can be safely given to people whose sole job is to maintain an instance.

### DBADM

DBADM, or Database Administrator, is the fourth of the available authorities. It is a database-level authority (not an instance-level one) and, again, can only be granted by SYSADM. DBADM authority applies to a specific database and entails the power to access and modify all the objects within it (tables, views, indexes and the kitchen sink so long as it is stored within the database).

The DBADM is often the person who looks after a database and has the power to undertake such tasks as inspecting log files, monitoring events, reorganizing tables and collecting statistics. In a small organization, this could easily be done by a SYSADM (who, as you've probably guessed, has all these powers too), but once a system grows and more than one database is in use, allocating a DBADM to each can be a useful step. Allocating two DBADMs to each database can be worthwhile, as redundancy is often beneficial, as mentioned above.

A DBADM can grant any privilege on an object in the database to any user and also grant other database-level privileges.

## Privileges

A privilege is a right to perform a specific action on a specific object in a database. Privileges can be (and usually are) assigned to groups, but they can also be assigned to individual users. A DBADM or SYSADM can allocate any privilege to any user or group.

❝ *You may find that some documentation for DB2 uses the term 'authority' in a rather less precise way than we use it here; in other words, we have seen the word used to mean 'privilege' as well as 'authority' (as defined above). It doesn't really matter how the words are used as long as the principle is clear.* ❞

The granting of each type of privilege simply controls what group members can do by giving them the right to perform a certain action. For example, by granting certain table privileges, a group might be allowed only to read the data in one table but to have read and modify rights in another. Privileges to do such things as add columns to a table, delete rows or create indexes can be bestowed or denied as deemed necessary.

When a database is created, certain privileges are granted automatically to all members of the group PUBLIC (which includes all users). These include:

- CREATETAB
- CONNECT

The first, CREATETAB, lets users create tables within that database, and CONNECT lets them connect to, and use, the database.

Different classes of object in a database have ranges of privileges associated with them. There are:

- database privileges
- schema privileges
- table and view privileges
- package privileges
- index privileges

Looking more closely at table and view privileges, for instance, we find that such privileges as:

CONTROL (a superset of the other table and view privileges)
ALTER
DELETE
INDEX
INSERT
REFERENCES
SELECT
UPDATE

are available.

The creator of a table is automatically granted CONTROL privilege, which is a superset of the possible privileges on a table or view. CONTROL is therefore the most powerful table or view privilege. With it you can add columns, delete rows, create indexes, update entries and so on, and even drop the table.

❖ *By 'superset' we mean that it includes all of the 'standard' privileges and also, for example, the ability to grant privileges associated with that table to other users.* ❖

The permutations of these privileges are vast, but despite this you should not find that allocating privileges takes much of your time. Those assigned by default are suitable for use in most cases. This overview will, we hope, give you an idea of the control you have over who can do what and to what.

## A Couple of Recommendations

We strongly recommend that you grant authorities to groups and not directly to individuals, though not simply for the administrative reasons described above. Granting DBADM (or any other) authority to a user will automatically grant a range of privileges to that user. So far, so good. However, if you then revoke that authority, the user will not lose those associated privileges unless they are *explicitly* removed from that user. On the other hand, suppose you grant an authority to a group. If you (or the NT administrator, see below) move someone into that group, that user gains the authority. If the user is moved out of the group, they lose both the authority and the associated privileges.

The only exception we would make to this is the user that we suggested you create in order to install DB2. This user is explicitly granted SYSADM authority by DB2. We strongly recommend that you keep this user on the system as a sort of super-SYSADM who can be used in emergencies.

We said that only SYSADM can grant authorities, and that is true, but remember that authorities and privileges are typically granted to groups and that DB2 uses NT groups. Put all of that together and you realize that SYSADM could assign, say, DBADM authority to a group called 'Penguin'. However, the NT administrator could then put another NT user into that group. In this case it could be argued that the NT administrator is actually granting DBADM authority. The semantics aren't particularly important; you just need to be aware that this is possible, and we recommend that SYSADM and the NT Administrator cooperate on security issues like this. (We know that these may actually be one and the same person, in which

## 8 • Users, Authorities and Privileges

case we hope that cooperation will occur naturally.)

# The Practical Bit

## Granting Authorities

As we said, DB2 makes use of NT groups. Suppose you intend to make use of three authorities – SYSADM, SYSCTRL and DBADM. While it isn't required, we recommend that you set up NT groups called by identical or similar names – SYSADM, SYSCTRL and DBADMSAM. (Database Administrator authority is applied to a specific database, so you may want to indicate the name of the database in the group name, as we have done.) The reason we suggest using identical or similar names is that it should then be clear to the NT administrator that anyone in the group SYSADM is going to have serious power within DB2.

Note that DB2 will only accept group names which are of eight letters or fewer, although the names of the users assigned to the group are not restricted in that way.

So, assuming that you have created the NT groups,

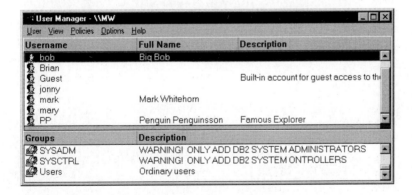

right-click on the instance called DB2 and choose Configure.

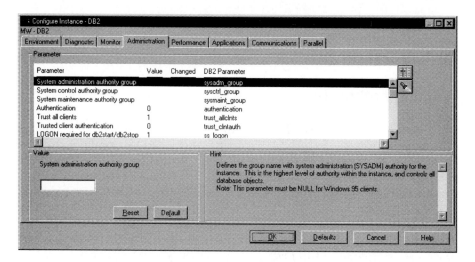

Select the Administration tab and you will see the three instance authorities. Fill in the names of the groups as appropriate

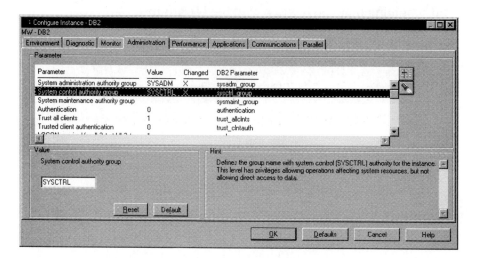

and then press OK.

To set DBADM authority, right-click on the relevant database (in our case, SAMPLE) and select Authorities. The dialog has two tabs; choose the one for Group.

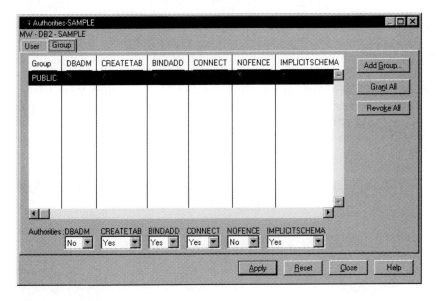

Click on Add Group, select the group you want (in our case DBADMSAM) and add it.

Then select the group and, using one of the appropriate buttons at the bottom of the dialog box, assign DBADM authority to the group.

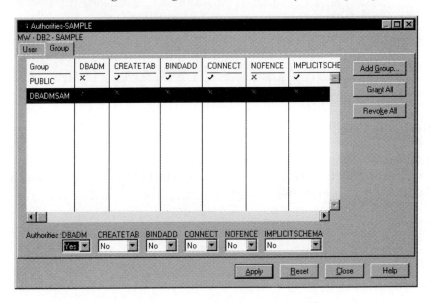

We said earlier that the term 'authority' is used in various ways in DB2, and here is an example. In this dialog box, DBADM is labeled as an authority – but so are CREATETAB, CONNECT etc., which we have referred to above as privileges. It doesn't really matter how you apply these words; what is important is that you understand what they do. Think of it this way: DBADM authority is a much greater power than any of the others listed in the dialog. You can see this in practice. When you grant DBADM authority to the group, you will find that the group automatically acquires all of the other privileges/authorities.

Finally click on the Apply button to apply that authority to the group.

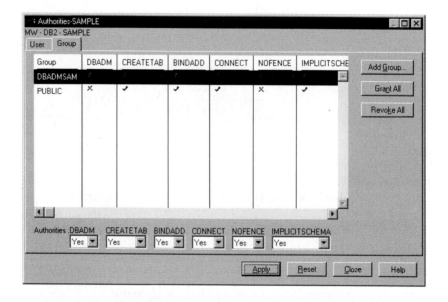

## Granting Privileges

Privileges are granted in one of two main ways.

Right-click on the object, such as a table, select Privileges and follow the dialogs for Add user or Add group.

## 8 • Users, Authorities and Privileges

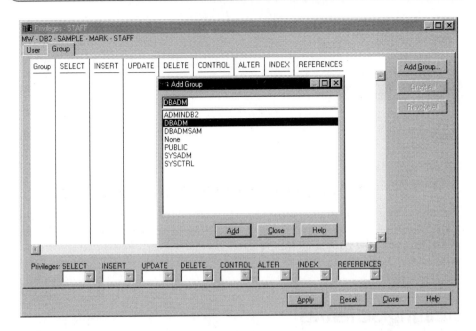

Or go to Groups, select a group and double click it. Then select, say, the Table tab, and alter the privileges using the combo boxes.

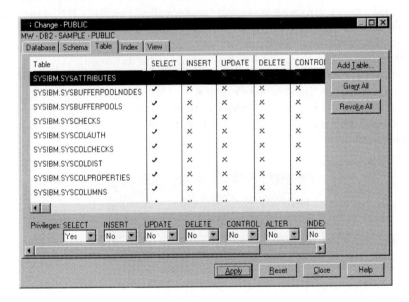

*Chapter 9*

# Schemas

Schemas: they keep on creeping into the screenshots and we keep on ignoring them – but no longer. Now is the time to expose schemas for the useful fellows that they are, busily providing a logical classification of the objects in a database.

## Creating Schemas

First of all, you will have noticed by now that every object in the database belongs to a schema. Schemas are, by default, named after the person who creates the object. Suppose you create a user called Penguin. If this user creates a table called HERRING, the table will belong to the schema Penguin. Indeed, if you then use the Control Center to examine the schemas you will find that one called Penguin has appeared in the database.

Thereafter, every object (table, view, index, trigger etc.) created by this user will belong to the schema Penguin.

You, as SYSADM, can also create schemas that have names other than that of your user ID. All you have to do is to right-click on Schemas in the object tree and type in the name.

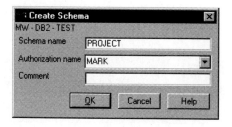

Schema names must begin with a letter and be eight characters or fewer in length, must not begin with SYS and must not already exist.

# 9 • Schemas

## What Use Are Schemas?

Schemas are part of the naming system for objects in the database. Thus a more complete name for HERRING is Penguin.HERRING. All of this is fine, but none of it answers the question 'What are schemas for?' If we can't find a benefit from using them, they are effectively functionless.

Start by imagining a database with only one user. In such a database schemas are effectively useless because, by default, every object will belong to the same schema. Now consider a database with several users all of whom have the right to create objects such as tables. If the database didn't support schemas, then as soon as one of them created a table called, say, STAFF, that would exclude any of the others from ever creating a table with the same name. Clearly, in a database the range of table names is huge. However, many will be very popular (EMPLOYEE, ORDER etc.) and without schemas there would be an unseemly rush to register the common ones as soon as the database was created. As it is, by default everyone gets their own schema, their schema name becomes part of the name of any object they create and all is well because DB2 sees Penguin.STAFF as a different object from King.STAFF and will allow both in the same database.

If you need further convincing, think about the people who develop DB2 applications to sell. How can they be sure that the names they choose for the (possibly) hundreds of objects in their database won't conflict with any existing objects in the (hopefully) hundreds of DB2 sites into which they hope to sell their application? Answer: by choosing an outrageous schema name. The tables and so on can then still have perfectly sensible names. Once you see schemas in this light, they make perfect sense.

Schemas can also be used to organize objects in the database and to ensure that the correct users have the correct power over those objects. A couple of examples may make this clearer.

❛ *Apart from SYSADM, most users can only have permissions to, say, drop a table if it is in their own schema. The implication is that if an object is in your schema, you created it, so you can drop it. (Remember that 'drop' in DB2-speak means remove, destroy, annihilate, obliterate.)* ❜

Now suppose you have a large project under way, and you want several of your users to be able to work on it together. You (as SYSADM) can create a schema called, say, PROJECT, and you can ensure that all of the users involved in the project have full access to the objects in the schema. Now any one of those users would be able to create tables in that schema. In addition, any of those users could drop any table in that schema, even if they hadn't personally created it.

The practicalities of allocating these 'rights' were discussed in the previous chapter (Chapter 8).

## Using Schemas

As SYSADM you have the power to create multiple schemas; you can also choose which objects go into which schemas, and who has which rights to each schema.

For instance, a view created for use by personnel services staff could belong to a schema called PERSERV and one created for administration staff could be called ADMIN. Both views can be of data in the same table, but the schema name indicates the users of each view and controls who can make use of it.

## Schema Names in Referencing Tables

We have created a schema name PROJECT in the database TEST. We have also created two STAFF tables in that database:

    PROJECT.STAFF
    MARK.STAFF

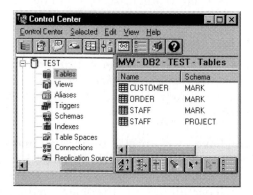

## 9 • Schemas

These two are clearly different:

| EMPLOYEE_ID | FIRST_NAME | LAST_NAME |
|---|---|---|
| 1 | Muriel | Owen-Pawson |
| 2 | Helen | Bayliss |
| 3 | Ken | Bayliss |
| 4 | Vicky | Bayliss |
| 5 | Sara | Bayliss |
| 6 | Jo | Bayliss |
| 7 | Sam | Dogman |
| 8 | Will | Dogman |

PROJECT_STAFF : Table

| STAFFID | FIRSTNAME | LASTNAME | ZONE | DEPTNUMB | STARTDATE | BIRTHDATE | DIVISION |
|---|---|---|---|---|---|---|---|
| 3 | Mark | Whitehorn | Purple | 4578 | 1/1/67 | 1/1/66 | MidWest |
| 4 | Marc | Whitehorn | Blue | 5445 | 1/1/78 | 1/1/68 | Eastern |

MARK_STAFF : Table

If we now connect to TEST and issue the command

```
SELECT * FROM STAFF
```

we get:

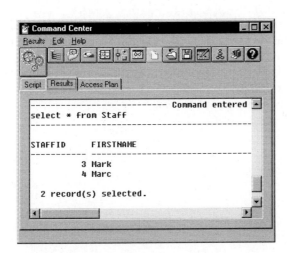

Despite appearances, DB2 didn't arbitrarily choose MARK.STAFF in preference to PROJECT.STAFF. We were logged in as MARK when we ran the SQL statement, and DB2 assumes that if you don't supply a schema name it should use your user ID.

If (still logged in as MARK) we use the longer form SELECT * FROM PROJECT.STAFF we get:

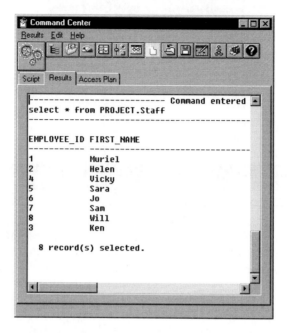

This has interesting implications when you are creating SQL statements, and the take-home message ought to be fairly obvious. If in doubt, use the schema name when referring to tables, since doing so removes ambiguity. This is particularly important when the SQL you (as DBA) are building is for general use (in views, triggers etc.), which leads us very happily to the next chapter, which is about Views.

*Chapter 10*

# Views

In a database, data is stored in tables. Permissions (as Privileges are sometimes called), which either allow or deny access, are given to users and groups of users for each table, as discussed in Chapter 8. Although the permissions can be varied for a given table (a user might be allowed to see the data but not edit it), they don't allow variation within a table. Thus a user can either see everything in a table or nothing and there are many occasions when this is far from ideal. Views provide a flexible way of letting users work with the data in a database.

Suppose you have a table of staff details. Clerical staff need to see data on the personnel employed (the department to which they're assigned, the date on which they started work and so on), but because the table also holds salary, performance and health records, unrestricted access cannot be allowed.

A view lets you provide clerical staff with access to the fields they need while maintaining the necessary security. It is also possible to create multiple views – one which allows personnel staff access to everything except medical details, and one for the medical officer which only allows access to medical records.

In many databases it is common to use controlled access to views as the *only* way in which users can access the data.

# 10 • Views

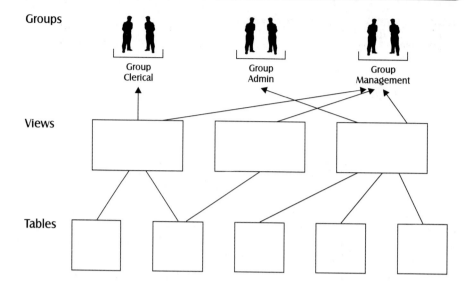

## Creating a View

We'll work with the SAMPLE database, so that you can try out the examples, and start with the EMPLOYEE table. It contains potentially sensitive material in the SALARY column, so we'll create a view of the table that only shows a subset of the columns.

In the Control Center, select the SAMPLE database. Right-click on Views and choose Create, which opens the Create View window.

You can specify the schema for your new view by selecting it from the View schema list box. If you don't, the view will take your user ID as the default.

Next you need to name the view, using between one and 18 characters. Note that the name must be unique within the defined schema, i.e. no other object in the schema can share the name. We called ours GENERAL (for want of anything better).

In the SQL statement box, an outline CREATE VIEW statement is already filled in, ready for the addition of a statement specific to the view you're creating. It looks like this:

```
[(columns, ...)]
AS [WITH (common_table_expression, ...)]
SELECT <columns>
FROM <tables>
WHERE <search_conditions>
```

## 10 • Views

To be brutally frank, we find this sort of presentation of information less than perfectly helpful – we find examples much more useful, so here's one:

```
(First, Last, Dept)
AS
SELECT FIRSTNME, LASTNAME, WORKDEPT
FROM EMPLOYEE
```

This works, and it says in English 'extract the three columns FIRSTNME, LASTNAME and WORKDEPT from the table EMPLOYEE. Display the contents of those columns but rename the columns as First, Last and Dept respectively'.

You can specify a Check option; this is optional, so leave it set at None for the moment. When you're building a production system, check options give finer control for verifying any insert or update operations that use a view.

Completing the subsequent Comment field is also optional. Clicking the OK button creates the view and lists it in the contents pane.

To see the result of creating this view, right-click the view and choose Sample contents.

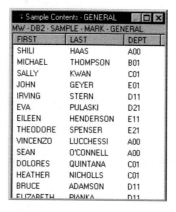

Subsequently, if you right-click on your view (in our case GENERAL) and select alter, you find that the SQL statement is not as you wrote it; it now reads:

```
CREATE VIEW MARK.GENERAL
(First, Last, Dept) AS
SELECT FIRSTNME, LASTNAME, WORKDEPT
FROM EMPLOYEE
```

Once the view has been created, you can treat it just like a table. For example, we used Access to display the view just as if it was a table.

# 10 • Views

When you create a view, you're building a 'virtual table' – there are no extra tables in the database when you've finished. It looks like a table, it smells like a table, but it isn't there really.

## What Distinguishes a View From a Query?

Clearly a view is based on SQL, which makes it look very much like a query. In fact, views share some characteristics with queries, so it is worth enumerating the differences between views and queries before we go any further.

- In general, DBAs create views and users create queries (clearly there are exceptions to this, but it stands as a general distinction).
- Views are stored in the database itself (in fact in the system catalog tables); queries are stored in the front-end application.
- Most importantly, the result set generated by a query is not updateable. The data displayed in a view is often updateable.

❝ *Exactly when the data in a view is updateable is a very complex issue, which happily falls outside the remit of this book. There is, however, a very pragmatic way in which you can determine whether a given view is going to be updateable – simply create it and then try to edit the data it contains. If you can do so then it is an updateable view.* ❞

## More Complex Views

The view we have just created simply restricts the number of columns that appear. It ought to go without saying (but we are far too unsubtle for that) that you can also restrict the rows that appear in a view; for example:

```
(First, Last, Dept)
AS
SELECT FIRSTNME, LASTNAME, WORKDEPT
FROM EMPLOYEE
WHERE WORKDEPT='D21'
```

Views have the added advantage of being able to hide the structure of the database from users, giving them a simpler interface with the data. Views can be created which pull together data from different tables, presenting users with what looks like a single table that contains everything they need for the task in hand.

The data in the WORKDEPT column tells us the department in which the employee works. The problem is that 'D21' or 'A00' is not very informative. The table DEPARTMENT lists all of these codes and also a name for each department – D21 is 'ADMINISTRATION SYSTEMS' and A00 is 'SPIFFY COMPUTER SERVICE DIV.' (*For which would you rather work?*)

If you type this into the view definition box:

```
(First, Last, Dept)
AS
SELECT MARK.EMPLOYEE.FIRSTNME,
MARK.EMPLOYEE.LASTNAME, MARK.DEPARTMENT.DEPTNAME
FROM MARK.EMPLOYEE INNER JOIN MARK.DEPARTMENT ON
MARK.EMPLOYEE.WORKDEPT = MARK.DEPARTMENT.DEPTNO;
```

a join is created between the two tables EMPLOYEE and DEPARTMENT and lists for us the department in which the employees work.

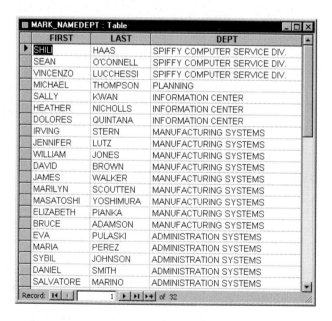

Which bring us to the subject of laziness. We didn't hand type this SQL: we used Access to create it for us. We set up links to EMPLOYEE and DEPARTMENT,

❢ *Note that Access automatically uses the schema name as part of the table name when the link is created.*

then we built a query that provided the information we wanted in the view.

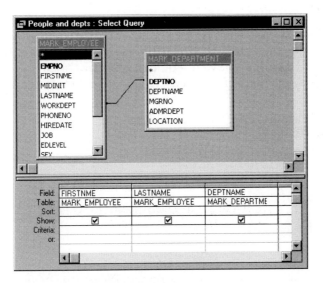

Once we were sure it was working we asked Access to show us the SQL.

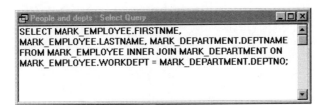

We cut and pasted that to a word processor, searched for '_' and replaced it with '.' and then cut and pasted the result into the view definition box. With a little bit of further judicious editing it was ready to roll. Of course, SQL being what it is (a very imperfect standard), some SQL statements may need more editing than others. Nevertheless, we find this an excellent way in which to generate the SQL we need in DB2.

As we said above, Access uses the schema name as part of the table name when the link is created. This happens to be very handy, because the simple search and replace described above leaves the schema names in place for the view. We strongly recommend that views are created using SQL which explicitly names the schemas, for reasons discussed in the previous chapter.

## Summary

Views are wonderful. You can use them, along with permissions, to provide exactly the correct information to precisely the right users. In addition, as our second example showed, you can use views to 'de-normalize' the version of the data that is presented to the user, making it clearer and more readable.

*Chapter 11*

# Backup and Recovery

❝ *Up to this point in the book we have tried to enumerate virtually every step you need to take in DB2 to perform the operations we are describing. From now on we will cut down the detail so that we can move faster. For example, DB2 asks you for a user ID and password during the backup process, but we don't bother telling you about this below because we assume that, by now, it is familiar to you.* ❞

At the simplest level, backup simply describes the process of taking a copy of your data and putting it 'somewhere safe'. Somewhere safe is typically defined as 'on some other medium such as tape and stashed in a fireproof vault under some large mountain range or other'.

Restoring a database is the process of getting the data back from its safe location and putting it on your operational machine.

Given a single-user machine that's only used for word processing, backup and restore are relatively easy to understand and perform. Given a multi-user system used for database applications, the processes become slightly more complex because there are more factors to be taken into account.

## Backups – a Couple of Definitions

### Off-Line

An off-line backup is the most straightforward. Ensure that no one is accessing the database (so that it is in a static state) and make a copy.

### On-Line

It is also possible to make an on-line backup, where users can continue to work with the database. It sounds very attractive (and it is) but more care needs to be taken when performing this, as described below.

## A Quick Start with the SmartGuides

IBM has provided SmartGuides for both backup and restore. Such a good job has been made of the SmartGuides that you can perform both operations without understanding the background factors. If you have installed the SAMPLE database, now is a good time to run through these SmartGuides.

### Backup SmartGuide

First, make sure that no one is currently using SAMPLE. One of the easiest ways of doing this, assuming that you are sure no one will be doing any serious work, is to go to the Control Center, right-click on the DB2 instance and select Force applications. This is brutal, because as the name suggests, it forces all of the applications for that instance (not just that database) off the system. It is therefore not normal practice on a live, working system, but should be fine if you are working with a test system. Then, in the Control Center, right-click on SAMPLE in the object tree and select Backup, Database using SmartGuide.

The SmartGuide opens at the Database page. This section lets you choose a database, but since you right-clicked on SAMPLE, that is selected by default.

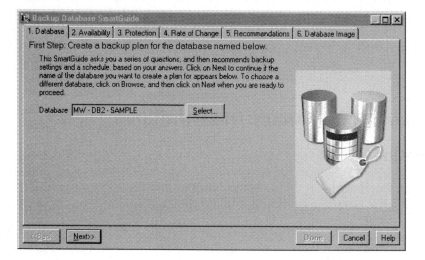

# 11 • Backup and Recovery

The next three tabs:

- Availability

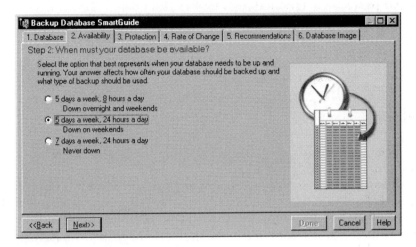

- Protection

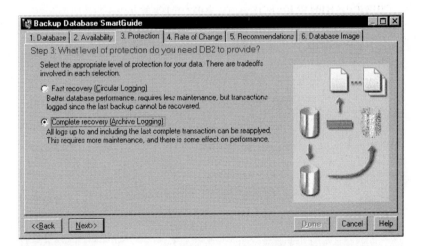

- Rate of Change

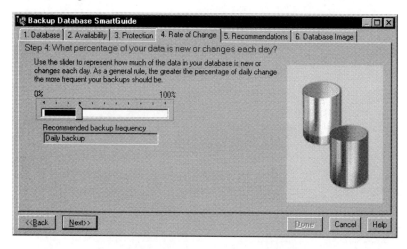

simply ask you about your database. The only suggestion we have is that you accept the default of Complete Recovery on page 3 unless you are very sure that you *don't* need it.

The SmartGuide needs this information in order to create the suggested backup strategy that is presented to you on page 5.

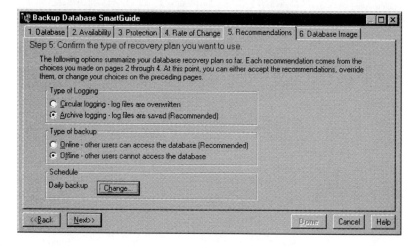

The information you supply will depend upon your data and database needs. You can alter the time (and frequency) of backups by clicking on the Change button:

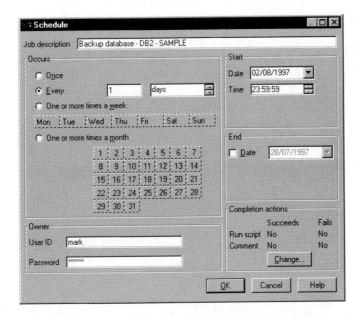

Once you are happy with the suggestions, on page 6 you can tell the SmartGuide where to put the backup.

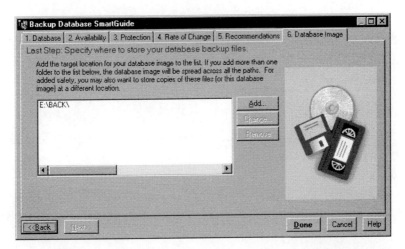

The SmartGuide supports disk and tape backup on Windows NT systems. If you have a tape drive fitted then we suggest you try backing up to that. Clearly, backing up to the same disk as the one holding the data is not as secure as backing up to a remote device (because if the disk goes down you're sunk) but it's OK for practicing.

We are sending this backup to another disk drive which is itself backed up once a day to tape (but don't think that we're paranoid or anything).

If you specify a subdirectory, say E:\BACK, then make sure you create E:\BACK before attempting to perform the backup, since DB2 won't create it for you and the backup will fail.

That's it. Press Done and the SmartGuide will do the rest. It has generated a Script, the existence of which you can verify by opening the Script Center:

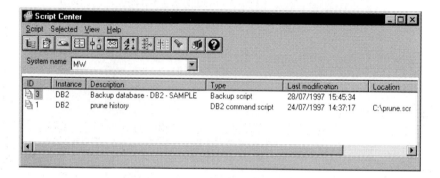

This script has also been scheduled for execution and you can check this in the Journal:

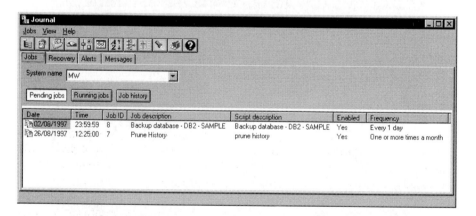

(If no jobs appear, make sure you have the correct system name selected.) We'll cover the Script Center and Journal in more detail in Chapter 12 on scheduling. However, for the moment you'll notice that, in the Journal, the backup is scheduled for every day at 23:59:59. In other words, although it will be done this evening, it hasn't actually taken place yet. Happily, you can force the backup to occur now, which will be useful since we can then demonstrate a restore. You can force a backup from

## 11 • Backup and Recovery

either the Journal or the Script Center, so open one of them now. Right-click on the backup job and select Run now.

If you are using a tape system, you may now have to carry out tape operations that will depend on the tape system you have installed.

After a brief pause, your backup job should be visible in the Job History part of the Journal and should be listed as Successful. (Try View Refresh if the status is Failed, then double click on the date stamp of the job and you should get a message telling you why the job failed. Try to fix the problem and then try to run the job again (it should still be in Pending).)

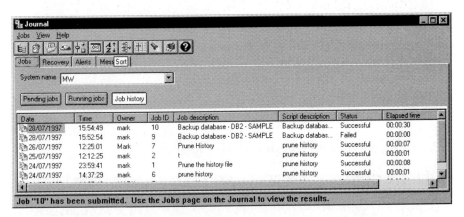

The first time we ran this job we purposely left a user connected to SAMPLE so that you could see what happens. The job (Job ID 9) failed as seen here. Once we had disconnected the user and rescheduled the job (Job ID 10), it ran perfectly.

## Restore SmartGuide (Recovery)

Before restoring the database, please use whatever front-end tool you favor to make a simple change to one of the records. The point of doing this will become clear as the restore proceeds, but in essence it is to ensure that the backup copy is now marginally out-of-date, so that you can see how well DB2 copes with that situation.

The Restore Database SmartGuide helps you restore a database (not unreasonably, given its name). In the Control Center, right-click the database to be restored and select Restore, Database using SmartGuide.

In page 1 the SmartGuide tells you what level of recovery is possible given your current backup settings, and page 2 shows the history of backups taken – you can choose the one from which to restore (typically the most recent).

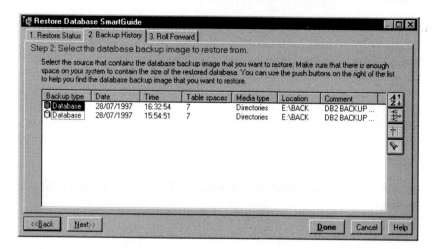

❥ We have taken another backup since the one described earlier so that you can see how more than one is presented. In practice, your screen should show only one. ❥

Page 3 is the only one you should need to alter.

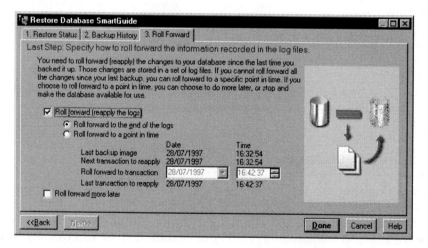

By default the SmartGuide restores your database to the state of the last backup. Since this could be several days old, it is likely that changes will have been made since then (and that is why we asked you to make a change). The option that you need to select on page 3 is Roll forward to the end of the logs. Logs are discussed below, but essentially they allow the changes made to the database since it was last backed up to be incorporated into the restored copy. You might wonder why this isn't the default: it's because the SmartGuide is being ultra-safe. We're not being ultra-safe, since we know you are working with non-critical data, so we can take the easiest option. Finally, click on the Done button.

As with the backup, the restore job will be scheduled, but in this case the job is scheduled for immediate execution and should complete very rapidly.

That's it. You have backed up a database and restored it. Congratulations!

You can now look in the database and you should be able to find the change that you made to the data after it was backed up. This doesn't mean that the restore didn't work; it means that DB2 restored the database from the backup and then reapplied the change that had been made since the backup. It can work this magic by using logs, which are discussed in some detail below.

> *You may now be wondering 'If I can do backup and restore without understanding the background, why should I bother reading the rest of this chapter?' The answer is that the more you know about backup and restore, the more you can configure your particular backup strategy to suit the needs of your business. Please, please read the rest of this chapter. It may help you to sleep better at night.*

## Why Back Up?

Isn't it intuitively obvious that you should back up your data? Apparently not. All of the RDBMS manufacturers that we know say the same thing: their work would be cut in half if all of their customers backed up their databases effectively. By the same token, it would save the customers a great deal of grief and aggravation as well.

During the research for this book we spent a week in Toronto, talking to the developers who were building DB2. We asked everyone we met 'What is the most important issue we should cover – Install? The Control Center? Java? What?'. Almost without exception they answered 'Backup'. The developers know that no matter how good their software is, once it is out there being used in the real world, too much is outside their control – power cuts, bad third-party applications, bad disks, bad memory – and all can screw up your data. A good backup strategy will protect it.

The data in a database is almost impossible to value precisely so its worth is often overlooked. If you find it difficult to calculate the value of your data, imagine that you create a database and use it successfully for a year. After the year is up, imagine that some undefined disaster destroys all the data. Now try to estimate three amounts:

- how much it would cost you to replace the data
- the value of business you would lose while the database was inaccessible
- the value of business you would lose in the future due to lost customer confidence

The sum of these three approximates to the value of the data. If the answer you get exceeds the cost of backing up then it is worth doing. If the answer is lower than that of backing up, then you don't have to worry about it (but you should now be wondering if it is worth building the database in the first place!).

In the following sections we will cover things which, although interesting in their own right, don't instantly appear to have much to do with the physical process of backing up (such as transactions). They do, however, have everything to do with how you should formulate your backup strategy.

## Transactions

Tables hold data, and that data is constantly being accessed, altered and updated by various operations. It is relatively common in certain applications for two or more of these operations to be logically related.

As an example, suppose Sophie gives Ross a check for amount X, written on her account, in payment for his Dodge Viper (Sophie has excellent taste in cars). Two discrete operations are involved. One is removal of amount X from Sophie's account; the other is the addition of the same amount to Ross's account. If the first operation succeeds and the second fails both parties are going to be upset (although Ross may be more vociferous).

> ❢ *There is an accidental pun in here. In the original draft of this book Sophie bought a Dodge Challenger but Mary suggested changing it to Viper because she liked that car better (I like them both so that was fine by me). Only at the proofreading stage did we remember that Microsoft's Transaction Server was code-named 'Viper'. Spooky, isn't it?* ❢

Logically related operations of this kind are called transactions.

When we send a transaction to a database one of three things can happen:

1. The entire transaction completes (in which case it is described as committed).
2. None of the transaction completes.
3. Part of the transaction completes.

Clearly, committing the transaction is the most desirable conclusion but, of the other two, it is far better if no part of the transaction completes than just some of it.

Typically, any one operation within a transaction is a single SQL statement; thus a transaction is usually made up of several SQL statements.

So that's a transaction, but why are they of such fundamental importance?

Transactions are usually generated by remote applications that send them to the RDBMS. If an application crashes during a transaction, the transaction may be left half completed; that is, the money has gone from Sophie's account but it hasn't arrived in Ross's. The database itself is fine in the sense that nothing has happened to offend its referential integrity. Both Sophie's and Ross's records show a balance in their current accounts; the problem is that the values it shows are inconsistent with reality. So, we need some mechanism for dealing with incomplete transactions.

## Rollback

Rollback means undoing the operations of a transaction that has not been committed. In other words, if a transaction fails to complete, rolling it back will leave the database in the same state it was in before the transaction started.

Rollback is amazingly useful because it can be used to deal with much more than just single applications that fail and leave one transaction uncommitted. Imagine a heavily used database running on a server that crashes (perhaps because the power goes down). If there were 50 transactions under way at that moment, the database is likely to be in a highly inconsistent state. However, if DB2 can roll back all 50 incomplete transactions, then it will be fine. Not only *can* DB2 do this, it will do it automatically for you whenever it is started up after a crash.

Clearly, in order to perform this magic DB2 needs to keep track of incomplete transactions, and this it does with logs.

## Logs

Whenever a transaction starts against a database, DB2 records the fact in a log file. Log files store information like:

- when a transaction starts
- what operations are completed
- when the transaction itself is completed (that is to say, committed)

The default form of logging in DB2 is known as Circular logging because of the way in which it is implemented.

## Circular Logging

As anyone who has worked with disk files knows, it is much easier to append information to a file than it is to delete particular pieces of information from within a file. Therefore DB2 doesn't actually remove references to committed transactions from the logs. Instead DB2 writes information to a log file until the file reaches a set size. (By default this is 1 Mbyte in DB2 for NT, but like virtually everything in DB2 it is configurable..) Thereafter DB2 opens a second log file, and writes the transactions into that. It also, of course, continues to note the completion of each transaction as and when it occurs. When that second file is full, DB2 opens a third. By the time *that* one is full, it is highly likely that every transaction recorded in the first file will have completed. If this is the case, DB2 recycles the first file. Thus at any time DB2 will typically have three log files in which it is recording the current transactions. Hence the term 'circular' logging, because typically three files are used in rotation.

A useful definition at this point is the term 'Active' log file. This describes a log file that contains references to one or more uncommitted transactions. Thus in the paragraph above we could have said 'By the time *that* one is full, it is highly likely that the first file is no longer active. If this is the case, DB2 recycles the first file'. The opposite of an active file is an inactive file, although the term doesn't seem to be used very much in practice.

Using circular logging, DB2 always has a full and complete record of all currently incomplete transactions, including the operations completed to date within each. If one transaction needs to be rolled back, DB2 has the necessary information in the active logs to do that. If the server on which DB2 is running crashes, when it is restarted it can examine the active logs and automatically roll back all of the incomplete transactions.

## Secondary Log Files

You may remember that we said above that DB2 maintains three log files and that by the time the third one is full the first is likely to be inactive. You might be wondering what happens if the first file *is* still active. All that happens is that DB2 opens a fourth log file, known as a Secondary log file (the default three are Primary log files). 'Yes, but what happens if...': then it opens a fifth. Clearly there has to be a limit somewhere, and there is. For the moment your databases are unlikely to need more that the default settings, and when they do you will find that DB2 allows you to configure them as you need.

## What is Stored in a Log File?

We said above that the log files store the 'operations' that are carried out during a transaction. This might imply that DB2 stores the actual SQL commands, since each operation is typically an SQL statement. However, this wouldn't work in practice. Consider the SQL statement:

```
UPDATE ORG
SET DIVISION = 'Western'
WHERE DIVISION = 'Eastern';
```

This statement looks for all records in the ORG table where the value in the column DIVISION is equal to Western and sets it to Eastern.

As supplied, the ORG table has three records in which DIVISION = 'Eastern' and two where DIVISION = 'Western'. After the SQL statement has run, there are five records where DIVISION = 'Western'. If all we have in the log file is the SQL statement and we try to roll back, how do we know which of the five to turn back to 'Eastern'? The answer is that we don't. So, in practice, the log file stores a copy of the information that is changed. However, if you imagine the log file as storing a set of 'reversible SQL statements', you have a perfectly functional mental picture of what it contains.

## Summary of Circular Logging

Maintaining circular logs clearly takes up resources, which is another way of saying that doing so must inevitably slow down the database slightly. However, the speed hit is tiny and the payoff is huge, since circular logging enables the database to roll back any or all incomplete transactions. In turn, the ability to roll back transactions enables DB2 to protect your database against corruption from:

- applications that crash
- server crashes

So circular logs are wonderful, but they don't protect your data against all possible disasters. For example, if the disk on which the database resides crashes, you still lose all of your data. This is, of course, where backup comes in. If you back up your database to disk every night, then if the disk crashes you can replace the disk and restore the database.

But suppose that the disk crashes at, say, four o'clock in the afternoon. You can restore the database to the state it was in the previous night, but you have lost all of this morning's transactions.

You can probably see where this is leading. Suppose you perform an off-line backup on Monday evening. On Tuesday morning, as transactions start to run against the database, you perform logging to ensure that you can roll back if necessary. However, instead of allowing DB2 to perform circular logging (which overwrites the inactive log files) you get it to keep all of the log files intact.

Now when the disk crashes at four o'clock, you replace it, restore the database, and then roll forward.

## Roll Forward

Running complete transactions from a log file against a backup is known as roll forward. (Clearly any uncommitted transactions in the log files are not run during a normal roll forward.)

Of course, as soon as you get the idea of roll forward, you realize that it has great potential. As long as the log files also contain a time/date stamp for each transaction, you can roll the database forward to any chosen point in time. So, if a rogue application (not to say a rogue employee) happened to be creating mayhem in your data for some time before the system finally crashed, you can roll forward to a point just before the damage started. Suddenly roll forward is a really powerful tool.

You can also use it as a form of archiving. Imagine you have a backup taken on 1/1/1998 and that you have log files for the next three months. If you wanted to see the state of the database on the 2/1/1998, all you have to do is to restore the database and roll it forward to the date you want.

❢ *It ought to go without saying (but we will say it anyway) that if your database was called, say, ADMIN, you would restore the backup to something called, say, ADMIN2 rather than overwrite your current copy of ADMIN!* ❥

This sort of roll forward is also known as point-in-time recovery.

This form of logging, where all of the log files are retained, can no longer be called circular logging and is referred to as Archive logging.

## Archive Logging

An archived log stores details of all transactions since the last backup and can be used to restore a database to any point between that backup and the failure (as described above).

When all the transactions in an active log are complete, the log is closed and, instead of being recycled as a new active log, it becomes an archived log.

It is worth explicitly stating that Archive logging doesn't prevent DB2 from being able to roll back transactions in exactly the same way as it could with circular logging. Think of archive logging as circular logging plus!

## Locations

Log files are kept on disk in the database log path directory. By default this is set to the same disk as the database. For performance reasons, you may well want to move it to another disk. In addition this can have positive data security implications; if the database disk melts down you don't lose the logs as well. You can't alter this using the SmartGuide and we haven't shown you how to make the change yet, but we will do so at the end of the chapter.

Really paranoid (sorry, really *careful*) DBAs will not only keep the log files on a different disk, they will periodically back up the inactive log files to yet another device (typically tape). This leads to yet another form of classification, because an archive log is described as 'on-line' when it is stored in the database log path directory and 'off-line' when it has been moved.

You can play games with these classification systems like asking if it is possible to have:

(a) an on-line active log file?
(b) an off-line inactive circular log?
(c) an off-line active log file?

Answers:

(a) Yes
(b) No
(c) No

## Backup Strategy

So, there is a whole host of options and possibilities. What we'll do now is to walk through the different options, pointing out their pros and cons.

When you create a database, DB2 applies circular logging by default. This keeps track of all the transactions that have been started but have yet to complete. Circular logging ensures that any or all uncommitted transactions can be rolled back if necessary. This protects your database against application failure, system crashes and power failure. In fact, this protection is automated. In the event of a server crash or power failure DB2 will automatically roll back uncommitted transactions whenever DB2 is restarted.

However, circular logging does not protect against media failure or, say, the actions of a disgruntled employee. For that you need archive logging.

Archive logging keeps copies of all transactions and allows DB2 to roll back uncommitted transactions as before, but also to roll them forward from a backup.

Since this sort of protection is valuable we make the following general recommendations for a production database. (You can be less particular for a test one, but we still recommend backing those up.)

## Recommendations

As soon as you create a database, and before you add data or let users loose on it, set the database log path directory to point to a disk other than the one on which the database resides. Run the backup SmartGuide and make an off-line backup of the database. At the same time, use page 3 of the SmartGuide to set Archive logging to on.

You now have a copy of the database on some other medium (presumably tape) and you have told DB2 to record every subsequent change to the database. These changes are being recorded away from the database. You are protected from transactions that fail to complete; in addition you should now be protected from a disk crash or an unhappy employee. Finally, we would suggest that you make backup copies of the on-line inactive log files on another medium, such as tape.

We've described what we hope is a safe strategy, but clearly only you can decide what is safe for your data. The information above is a broad overview that should help you to determine your own backup policy.

❢ *Incidentally, we say that you should put the log files on another disk, but that disk should be located on the same server, not a remote one. The problem with using a remote server is that, should the network glue up (or fail completely) your database will run abysmally slowly or die.* ❡

## Other Points Worth Considering

### Backup SmartGuide

The backup SmartGuide is very good and is well worth using. The first time it runs it will generate a script. That script is run at regular intervals by the Journal. If you decide to run the SmartGuide again it will generate another script, but it won't delete the first. So, if you use the backup Smart-Guide more than once for the same database, you will have to do some script housekeeping.

By default, the restore SmartGuide leaves a database in roll forward pending state, meaning that the database is restored but *not* rolled forward (see the section below on Configuring Backup Parameters). This is the safest option. Imagine that an application has spent the last three days sending transactions that have subtly mangled your data. The last thing you want the restore SmartGuide to do is to repeat all of these transactions. However, if you restore a database without doing anything about roll forward you will find that you can't use it at all because DB2 will consider it to be in roll forward pending state. The easiest approach is to make up your mind what you want to do about roll forward before you do the restore and then get the restore SmartGuide to do it.

## Off-Line Backups

An off-line backup is the most straightforward. Ensure that no one is accessing the database (so that it is in a static state) and make a copy.

## On-Line Backups

It is also possible to make an on-line backup, where users can continue to work with the database. An on-line backup isn't a snapshot of the database at an instant of time. Instead, it may be spread over several minutes, hours or even days. Note that an on-line backup is highly likely to contain inconsistent data because some transactions will have started before the backup and will complete during it. Others will start during and complete afterwards. An on-line backup is thus of little value if archive logging isn't in operation. On the other hand, if archive logging *is* running then the backup is perfectly valid – *as long as* you roll the database forward to a point in time that is after the end of the backup.

As general advice, use off-line backups if possible; they generally make your life easier.

## Restore Database Recovery History

The Journal has a page entitled Restore Database Recovery History, in which is shown the backup log of the database with which you are working. This can be very handy if you lose track of what you have done with a database. No chance of that happening, we know, but still....

## Roll Forward Pending

If you ever find that you cannot connect to a database because it is in Roll forward pending state, right-click on the database and investigate the option called Roll-forward.

## Configuring Backup Parameters

Finally, an important bit, not only for backing up but for other areas too.

Hopefully, you believe us that the log files are very important. We said earlier that you could configure parameters such as the number of secondary logs. What we haven't done is tell you how to do it. Now's the time.

The process described below not only works for changing the parameters of log files, it also gives you access to many other parameters for editing, including those for environment and performance settings.

To configure any parameters, right-click on a database (SAMPLE, for instance) and choose Configure from the menu. A Configure database window opens, its pages offering a choice of six types of parameter from which we'll choose Logs.

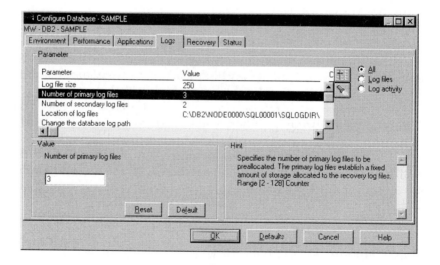

You can now scroll through the list of parameters, using the radio buttons for looking at log files and log activity separately (or together), to find the ones you want to tweak. Beneath the window showing the parameters are two further windows; on the right are helpful hints, and on the left is where you edit the parameters. There's a handy Default button for resetting things after experimentation.

## 11 • Backup and Recovery

We mentioned that the default number of primary log files is three, and you can see this by scrolling to the Number of primary log files entry. Sure enough, the value is set to 3. If you require more files, increase the number. The log file size is shown as 250, which means that each log file will consist of two hundred and fifty 4 kbyte pages; thus each file is 1 Mbyte. We also mention the database log path above; this is shown under Location of log files.

*Chapter 12*

# Scheduling Tasks

## Why Schedule?

DB2 provides the necessary tools to let you determine exactly when tasks will be performed. The ability to schedule is vital if you are to make efficient use of the system during quiet periods (during the early hours of the morning is often a useful slot) for housekeeping, gathering statistical information and the all-important backing up process. Such jobs can be run automatically and unattended while you sleep the sleep of the organized.

One example of scheduling has already been illustrated using the Backup Database SmartGuide; once the strategy has been specified, you can use the scheduler to arrange a time at which the backup will take place. The job appears automatically in the Journal, which is a tool for inspecting jobs that have taken place, are taking place or will take place in the future.

## Scripts

It is also possible to create scripts that can be scheduled in the same way. A script is a stored series of SQL statements, DB2 commands and/or operating system commands created in the Command Center or in the Script Center. Each script is like a tiny application that can be used time and time again.

Examples of jobs that are suitable for scheduling include:

- backup;
- prune history;
- running a query that stores the results in another table for later perusal.

We'll use Prune history as the example, since it allows us to introduce the topic of the recovery history file.

DB2 maintains a recovery history file which contains a record of all backup and restore operations performed on a database. By default this information is kept for 366 days (you can configure that value as described at the end of Chapter 11. Just choose the Recovery tab rather than the Logs tab).

However, you can manually prune the history file – that is, trim away all entries before a specified date. The command to do this is the delightfully named 'Prune History'. If you wanted to do this periodically, you could save the necessary commands into a script. You could then edit the date (and possibly the database name) whenever you wanted to prune a history file.

## Creating and Scheduling a Job

We'll walk through the process of creating, saving, scheduling and executing a script, starting with writing a script in the Command Center.

Open the Command Center and click the Script radio button. This means the commands you type will not be executed immediately; the alternative is Interactive, which runs each command when you press Ctrl+Enter.

Create a simple script, such as:

```
Connect to SAMPLE
Prune history 19970101235900
Connect reset
```

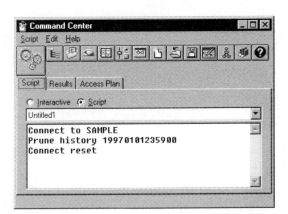

❻ *This example file removes all entries in the history file for SAMPLE which are time-stamped prior to 01/01/1997 @ 23:59. This is perfectly safe for the SAMPLE database in a test system. Please don't trim the history files of any production databases unless you are sure you know what you are doing. If you do absent-mindedly trim away the entire history file for such a database, restoring that database becomes by no means impossible, but slightly more involved.* ❾

Choose Save as from the Script menu. Where you save the script and with what extension is up to you. We have elected to save it in `C:\Sqllib` with the extension `.SCR`.

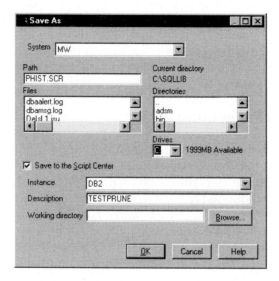

We recommend that you leave Save to the Script Center checked, so that when you open up said Script Center:

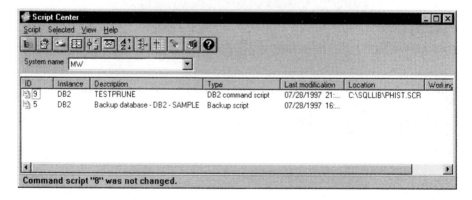

your script will appear. It is (hopefully) clear that scheduling a prune history script to run multiple times is a little pointless, but it will serve fine for demonstration purposes.

To schedule it, click on it with the right mouse button and choose Schedule from the pop-up menu. Make your choices of date, time and frequency in the Scheduler; you can also define a completion action that can be a message issued on completion. You could also choose to run another script if the first one completes successfully, and a different one if it fails, but we'll stick with just a completion message. Click OK when you've finished.

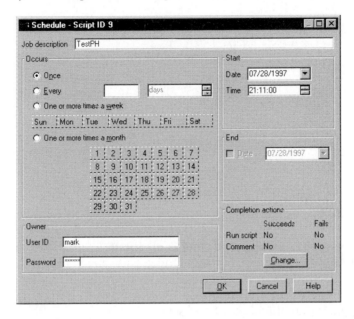

We've scheduled ours to run in a couple of minutes to make sure it works.

Now go to the Journal, where your scheduled script, rejoicing in its new status as a job, is listed as a pending job.

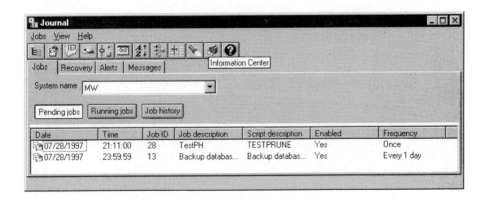

# 12 • Scheduling Tasks

Once the time has passed, the job should appear in Job History.

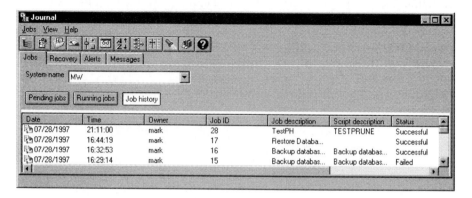

## Summary

That, in essence, is what scheduling is all about. Clearly, the most likely candidate at first is backup. However, once you start to use DB2 it is likely that you will find tasks that need to be carried out at regular intervals. That's the time to turn to the manuals, work out which DB2 commands are required, put them into a script and schedule it.

*Chapter 13*

# Triggers

A trigger can be thought of as a very small program that is set to go off under certain conditions. (Or, less prosaically, think of a trigger as a loyal servant who watches for certain events and, when they occur, carries out your bidding.) The 'program' is one or more SQL statements, and a trigger is activated by one of three types of modification to a table, namely the SQL statements:

- `DELETE`
- `INSERT`
- `UPDATE`

Triggers can be used for many things (limited only by your imagination really), but they are often used for data integrity checking. They offer a level of integrity control that goes beyond that which is possible with check constraints, which can only operate within a single table.

Business rules (also part of integrity checking) can also be enforced with triggers. Imagine you had a table of salary data and that you update an employee's salary from grade 1 to grade 2 on a scale. A trigger can ensure adherence to a business rule that states that an employee at grade 1 must have been employed at that grade for $x$ years before being eligible for advancement. More excitingly, triggers can even be used to send out email notifications under certain conditions, like the arrival of a particular value in a table. Perhaps your company has just taken its 1000th order and a party is called for. A trigger could have been set to detect this event which sends an email ordering champagne. (As a purely personal preference, we see more merit in the latter trigger than the former.)

## Trigger Terminology

A trigger has a name comprising a schema name and a trigger name. The schema name, as usual, will be your user ID by default.

As we said above, a trigger has a triggering operation (i.e. the event that sets it off) which is a DELETE, INSERT or UPDATE statement.

A trigger has an activation time (i.e. the time when it's set off) which can be either before or after a DELETE, INSERT or UPDATE statement, giving six possible combinations. Terms such as 'Before trigger' or 'After UPDATE trigger' are often used to describe the various types that can be built.

A trigger also has 'granularity'. Any SQL statement that triggers a trigger may insert, delete or update one or more rows. If it affects multiple rows then an interesting question arises. Should the trigger fire once, or once for every row that is affected by the SQL statement? The answer is that you can opt for either by specifying the granularity.

A trigger that fires only once for each SQL statement is known as a Statement trigger, while one which fires for every row that is affected is referred to as a Row trigger – sensible names really. This granularity means that triggers can be described as 'Statement triggers', 'After INSERT Row triggers' etc.

You will have noticed that the classification of triggers is becoming a little tortuous, since we have three different systems of description:

- DELETE, INSERT or UPDATE
- Before or After
- Row or Statement

There are certain restrictions that are placed on the possible combinations. For example, After triggers can be either Row or Statement triggers, but Before triggers can only be Row triggers. *You will probably be as delighted as we were to discover that the Create Trigger dialog grays out the impossible combinations.* These restrictions can be seen as just that – restrictions. On the other hand, they can be seen as useful indicators that illustrate the real differences between the way in which Before and After triggers are typically used.

## Typical Usage of Before and After Triggers

In general, Before triggers are used to ensure that all is well before a change is made to a row. Think of a typical Before trigger like this – it says 'Before you make this change, check this fact'. If the fact proves to be false, the SQL which triggered the trigger will be rolled back.

In general, you would use After triggers when you are happy that a particular operation is acceptable and you want some other operation to follow it.

What we need here is a couple of examples.

## Before

Imagine that the CEO of your company decides that no customers can be deleted from the database if they owe your company money (sounds sensible to us). Here you would use a Before trigger – 'Before you delete this row, check that the customer is credit-clean and don't allow the deletion if the customer is in our debt'.

## After

Imagine that you want to keep a count of the total number of customers somewhere. In other words, if you add a customer to a table, you want to increment a counter in another table. In this case you don't want to prevent the SQL which is performing the Insert, you just what to increment the counter when it runs. In this case, you would use an After trigger.

Now comes the tricky one. You remember that there is a restriction that says you can't have a Statement Before trigger. In other words, you can't have a trigger that runs once and only once before an SQL statement that could, potentially, affect multiple rows. The reason may now be slightly clearer. Before triggers are typically used to protect individual rows from unacceptable changes. Since a Statement trigger can't 'protect' individual rows, it is not allowed.

## More About Triggers

A trigger has a body. This is an important bit, the part that determines what a trigger will do when the conditions that fire it are met, and it comprises one or more SQL statements.

A trigger can have conditions that determine whether the trigger body is executed or not. If you only want the trigger to run if, say, the new employee that you are inserting into a table is in a particular department, you add a condition to this effect. Defining a condition for a trigger is optional.

Triggers are potentially very secure devices. They can enforce business rules at table level, even if you use a range of front-ends. A trigger is attached to the table, and will fire regardless of the front-end application which initiates the trigger event. Tables can have multiple triggers attached to them, and if triggers share a triggering event and activation time, they will be activated in the order in which they were created.

If this all sounds as if we are enthusiastic about triggers, that's because we are. We could almost, at this point, start to paraphrase A. A. Milne...

# 13 • Triggers

*'The wonderful thing about Triggers
Is Triggers are wonderful things'*

...but we won't.

## Create Trigger Dialog

OK, that's the end of theory (and the poetry). Now is the time to look at creating a simple trigger to see how they are used in practice.

We'll build one which increments a counter of the number of employees whenever a new employee record is added. It will be attached to the EMPLOYEE table in the SAMPLE database. The trigger will be activated after an INSERT operation and will work for every row modified. It is therefore an After INSERT Row trigger.

In order to make this work we will, of course, need a table in which to store this counter. So, use the Control Center to create a table called COMPANYINFO which has a single column called NOEMP that can be of type Integer. To keep this realistic, you might want to insert the value 33 (which is the current number of employees) into this column.

Right-click on Triggers in the object tree for the database SAMPLE and choose Create.

In the Trigger tab, select the trigger and table schema as appropriate, type in a name for the trigger itself and choose to attach it to the EMPLOYEE table. Click the After and the Insert radio buttons.

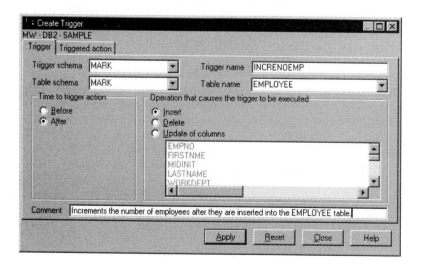

## 13 • Triggers

Move to the Triggered Action tab and click the Row button. In the Triggered Action box, a template of SQL statements is shown:

```
WHEN ( search-condition )
BEGIN ATOMIC
triggered-SQL-statement ;
END
```

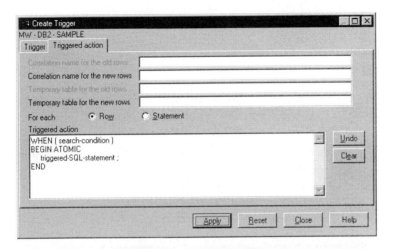

which can be edited or deleted as you wish. In our case, all we want the trigger to do is to increment the value in NOEMP that is contained in the table COMPANYINFO. So the statement we need is standard SQL, namely:

```
UPDATE COMANYINFO
SET NOEMP=NOEMP+1
```

So, this can replace the template:

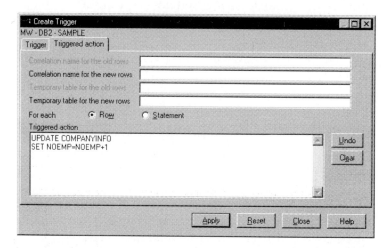

If you want your trigger to fire only when certain conditions are met, add the necessary search conditions after the WHEN statement, which must come before the triggered action statements.

Press the Apply button to set the trigger, and then close the dialog box. At that point the trigger should be listed in the Control Center.

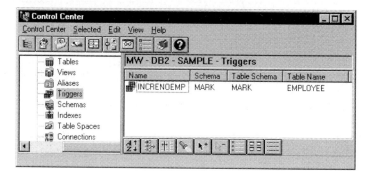

## 13 • Triggers

You can double-click it to view how it has been set.

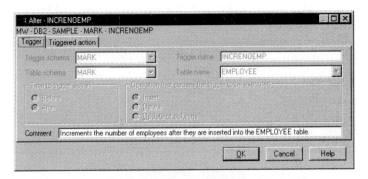

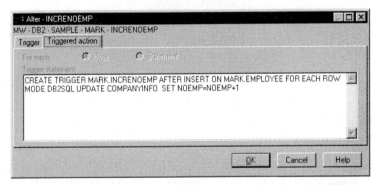

Note that DB2 has rewritten your statement to create a full DB2 command for creating the trigger you specified.

Finally, of course, you will want the fun of testing this trigger to see if it works.

Here are the tables before we start adding employees:

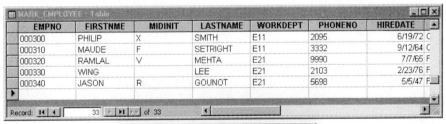

## 13 • Triggers

And here are the same tables after two employees have been added and the tables 'refreshed' in Access (in other words, closed and reopened):

| EMPNO | FIRSTNME | MIDINIT | LASTNAME | WORKDEPT | PHONENO | HIREDATE |
|---|---|---|---|---|---|---|
| 000310 | MAUDE | F | SETRIGHT | E11 | 3332 | 9/12/64 |
| 000320 | RAMLAL | V | MEHTA | E21 | 9990 | 7/7/65 |
| 000330 | WING |   | LEE | E21 | 2103 | 2/23/76 |
| 000340 | JASON | R | GOUNOT | E21 | 5698 | 5/5/47 |
| 000350 | SALLY | R | JONES |   |   |   |
| 000360 | BRAIN | R | SMITH |   |   |   |

Record: 33 of 34

NOEMP: 35

You would, of course, have to write more triggers in order to keep this figure in COMPANYINFO accurate (such as a DELETE trigger) but this, hopefully, gives you some idea of how to use triggers in DB2. In fact, triggers are a rich field and will repay more detailed study as your databases become more complex.

❻ *This exercise may seem a little odd, since you can query the EMPLOYEE table at any time to recover the value recorded in COMPANYINFO. However, imagine your company had 10 different tables of people it employed in different roles and locations. Each table could have this type of trigger attached, updating a single counter which would therefore be a total count of all employees.* ❾

*Part 3*

# Advanced Features

Chapter 14

# Monitoring DB2

DB2 provides several 'monitoring' systems that will help you to get the best from your system. These run in the background and collect information that is then analyzed, either by DB2 itself or by you, to gain an overview of how a system is performing. Studying this information can help you detect potential problems, let you analyze trends in the performance and tune the configuration parameters accordingly. It also helps analyze the performance of database applications.

The two main tools are Snapshot Monitoring and Event Monitoring. Both are wonderfully versatile and configurable, and here we can only show you a tiny portion of their capabilities. We'll explain what they do and illustrate a simple example upon which you can expand when you wish to bring their power to bear on your own system.

## Event Monitoring and the Event Analyzer

Events are things that happen to databases, and event monitoring can be used to trace many of these activities. You can create your own event monitors to observe that which interests or concerns you. For instance, you might set up an event monitor if one user complains of slow access to a particular table while others report a fast response, or if you wanted to track a particular user's activity. The event monitor generates records of the information you need, whether for performance or security reasons.

When an event monitor is running, data is collected in a continuous stream from events as they happen and is directed to a file. Once the monitoring is complete, the contents of the file are ready for inspection with the Event Analyzer.

Event monitors work within a single database, and events such as those below can be monitored and the results viewed with the Event Analyzer:

- database connections and disconnections
- transactions
- SQL statements
- deadlock activity

It sounds wonderful and it is, but there is no such thing as a free lunch. Intensive monitoring can put a heavy extra load on the system, so use it sparingly.

## Setting up an Event Monitor

Right-click on a database object in the Control Center (how about SAMPLE?), choose Monitor events, and a blank Event Monitors window opens. Click on Event monitor in the menu and choose Create.

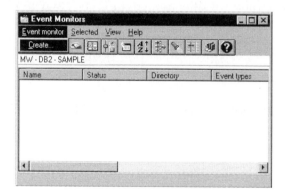

The next screenshot shows the dialog in which you define your event monitor. We've called ours Penguin, and it will monitor connections, transactions and statements. Each of these events can have a filter, and we've set all three to monitor the activity of a user with the authorization ID of MARK (a suspicious user if ever we saw one). The filter must be set for each event; you could, if you wished, monitor connection events for one user, transaction events for a second and statement events for a third.

## 14 • Monitoring DB2

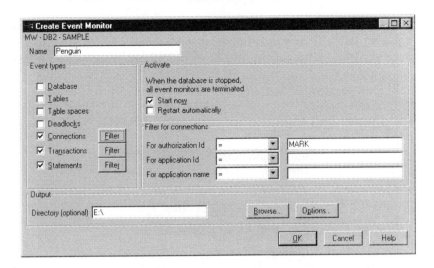

There isn't much information on the types of event in this dialog, but dipping out to read the available help is worthwhile.

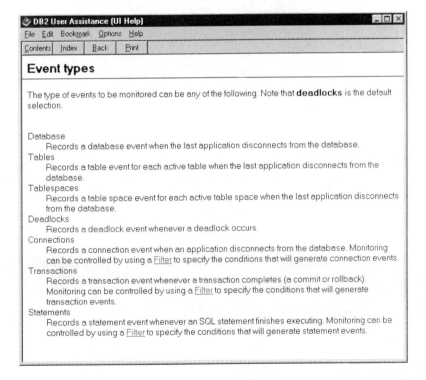

The event monitor is set to start as soon as it has been defined. It will run until you turn it off or until the database becomes inactive. When the database becomes active again, monitoring will not restart automatically (unless you check the appropriate box).

Finally, we've directed the output to E:\ – normally you would accept DB2's default – but we've sent it to E:\ for ease of demonstration.

A click on the Options button

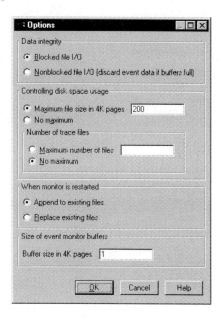

opens up a whole collection of further settings with which you can play. We'll stay with the default settings, so click Cancel to return to the Create Event Monitor window. Click on OK when you've finished and a message should tell you that the event monitor has been created successfully.

You'll now see, in the Event Monitor window, that an event monitor called Penguin has been started.

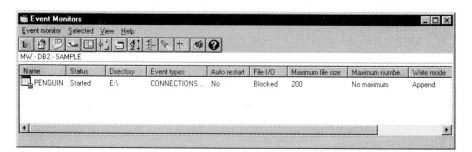

## 14 • Monitoring DB2

Now go and initiate a few events. From the Control Center, right-click on a table object and look at its sample contents, connect to a table with Access, edit a record and disconnect again – just do a few things likely to generate the events you're monitoring.

We could, at this stage, look at the files that have been created on E:\ but we've found that the file size is not necessarily indicative of the amount of activity because the writes to the file are buffered. Instead, we'll return to the Event Monitor, right-click on Penguin and select Stop event monitor; sure enough, the status of Penguin is now stopped.

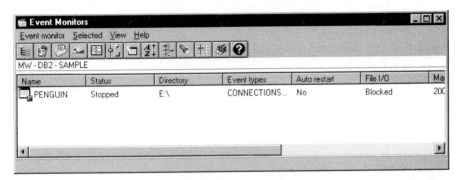

Now we'll have a look at the files generated on the E: drive: there are two of them, called `db2event.ctl` and `00000000.evt`. Typically you wouldn't bother looking for these, but we find it adds a little to the overall picture of what's going on.

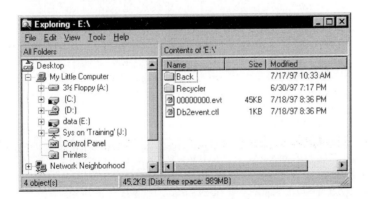

Return to the Event Monitor, right-click on Penguin and choose to View event monitor files. There's one shown; right-click on its Start Time and choose Open as and then Connections.

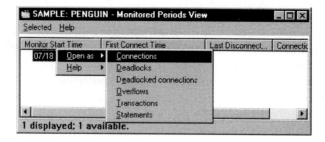

The Connections view shows all sorts of details about the connections made during the time the monitor was running,

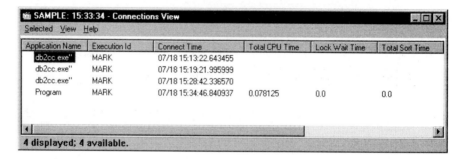

and if you choose Open as, Transactions, you'll see a list like this:

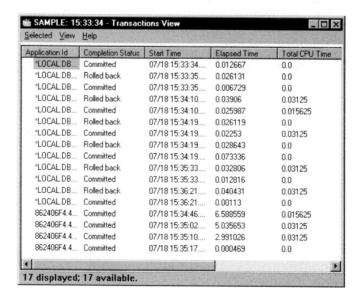

The Open as, Statements view looks like this:

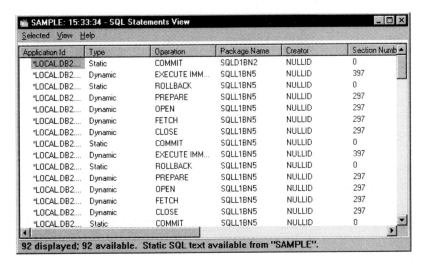

If you choose Open as, Deadlock, Deadlock connections and Overflows, you'll probably see that none occurred, but this does not mean they are unimportant; it's more of an indication of the simplicity of the example we suggested you perform. Information on such events can be vital for troubleshooting production databases.

You can define up to 32 event monitors at any one time, which should generate enough information to keep you busy for a good while.

## Snapshot Monitoring

Snapshot Monitoring and Event Monitoring sound similar, so we'll try to distinguish them.

The Snapshot Monitor is used to display information about the database in (more or less) real-time, as opposed to Event Monitoring, which logs information for later study.

Suppose your database, which has been well behaved up until now, starts running at about the speed of cold molasses – is it because the number of connections to the database has gone through the roof, or because multiple complex queries are being run against it? You can use a snapshot monitor to look into this. Note that this example is a good distinguisher between event and snapshot monitoring. With an event monitor you could log every time a given user connects to the database, but you couldn't tell how *many* were connected at the *same* time. The Snapshot

Monitor can't tell you if user X is connected, but it can tell you minute by minute how many users are connected.

If you right-click on, say, the ORG table in SAMPLE and choose Snapshot Monitoring, you will find a sub-menu with four options.

We are going to define what these mean because we found the menu somewhat confusing at first.

- *Start monitoring*
  This means start actively monitoring this particular object, i.e. 'look at a variety of parameters at regular intervals and be prepared to display them'.
- *Stop monitoring*
  Means stop actively monitoring this particular object.
- *Show monitor profile*
  Has nothing to do with this particular object at all. It means 'take me to your leader'. (*OK, we just slipped that in to see if you were awake.*) It means 'take me to a dialog box where I can look at the overall monitoring process'.
- *Show monitor details*
  Means 'Show me the information that can be monitored about this item in real time, on the screen, now'. An important point is that selecting this option also starts the monitoring process for this particular object. This is implicit, since it would be impossible for DB2 to show you the values without starting the monitoring process, but we feel it is worth stating implicitly. (This is another way of saying that the fact escaped us the first time around and we spent some time figuring it out!)

The first two options (Start and Stop monitoring) have no immediately visible effect.

The third option, Show monitor profile, opens this dialog box.

# 14 • Monitoring DB2

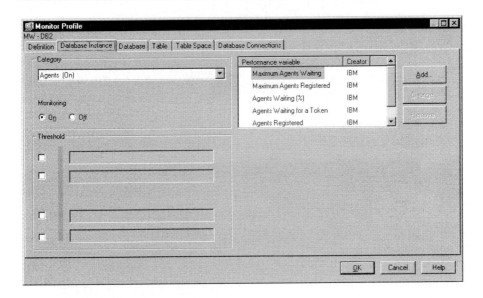

This is the heart of the Snapshot Monitor because it shows every performance variable that can be monitored. As you can see, these are subdivided into Database Instance, Database etc. Click on any of the tabs and you can browse through the possible variables that are monitorable. If you are a hardened DB2 professional from another platform you will instantly recognize most of these. If not, most will be unfamiliar, but it is comforting to know that, when you need to monitor some aspect of DB2's behavior, the tools are there to do it. *In fact, you can actually create your own variables with the Add button, but we'll leave that for another book!*

Not all of the variables are esoteric. For example, if you select the Database tab and choose Connections from the Category combo box, you'll see that you can monitor the number of current connections to the database (in three different ways!).

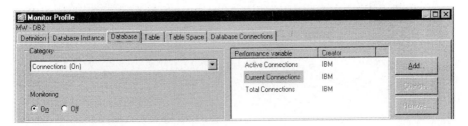

Under Tables, you can monitor the number of rows read from a table per second.

209

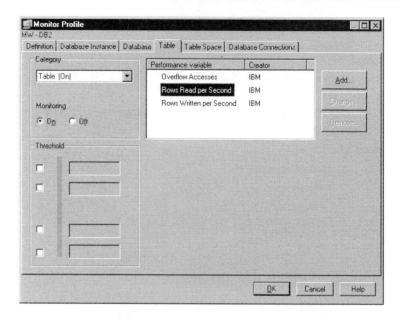

So there are lots of things that you can monitor, but how do you go about it? Simple. Suppose we decide to monitor the rows read from a table and want DB2 to alert us if the number exceeds a certain value. Select the Table tab, highlight Rows Read per Second and then turn your attention to the Threshold part of the dialog.

Click the uppermost check box and the following dialogs appear.

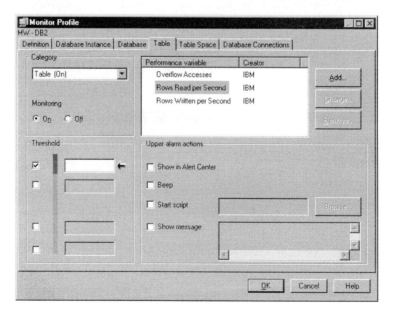

If you make the selections as follows:

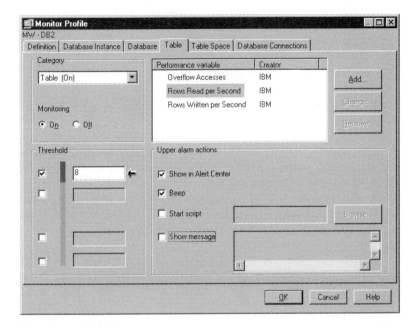

you are telling DB2 to:

- Keep watch on the number of reads per second
- If the number reaches or exceeds 8 per second, it is to make a beeping sound and place a message in the Alert Center.

❢ *Incidentally, we are certainly not suggesting that eight rows read per second is likely to be a cause for concern in a real database; we are just using that low value for demonstration purposes.* ❡

You can also tell DB2 to show messages and/or fire a script. Since scripts can do virtually anything (from running SQL to sending email) the possibilities are endless.

You can set two 'upper thresholds': a red one (dark grey in the figure) shown and a yellow one (light grey).

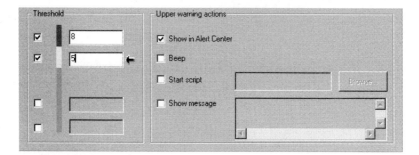

The highest one is typically used for alarms and the lower one for warnings. In other words, if you are interested in a performance variable you can have DB2 warn you when the level is creeping up and perform a specific action when the level gets critical.

You can also set lower level thresholds ('when a performance variable falls below this value, take this action').

In the definition tab you can set the interval at which monitoring takes place.

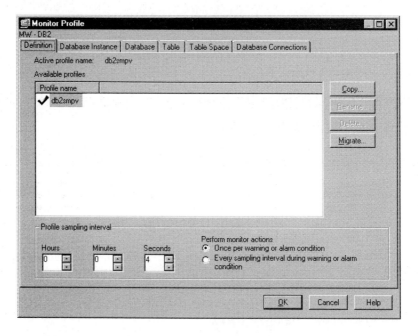

Remember that monitoring places a load on DB2, so you need to think about this seriously in a production database. However, for testing we have set it down at 4 seconds.

Once you have done all of that, press OK.

## 14 • Monitoring DB2

Now, if you use your favorite front-end tool to access the database and you start opening and closing tables (which will cause rows to be read)... absolutely nothing happens.

Strange, that. After all, you have set up a table monitor that is supposed to beep the server and send a message to the Alert Center whenever more than eight rows are read from a table per second. You are reading more than that, but nothing happens. The answer lies in the fact that the Monitor Profile is used to define *how* a performance variable is to be used. What it doesn't define is which table(s) should be so monitored. Since we haven't explicitly told it which to monitor, none is being monitored. In a production database you might have hundreds of tables. Do you really want them all to be monitored at the same time? (Doubtful.) So, the Monitor Profile says *how* (in this case) the rows read from tables should be monitored, but not *which* tables should be monitored.

So, right-click on the ORG table in the control Center, select Snapshot monitor and Start monitoring. Then try opening and closing the table a few times in rapid succession, and you should get an earful of beeps and multiple messages in the Alert Center. You have to be quick because an alert only lasts while a threshold is exceeded; if an alert is triggered by a value in one snapshot but that value reverts to a normal level by the time the subsequent snapshot is taken, the alert disappears from the Alert Center. The good news is that alerts are also logged automatically in the Alerts page of the Journal, so that a complete history of alerts and warnings is available.

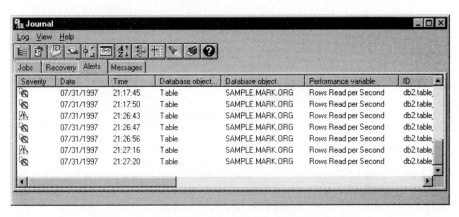

You can also watch as the data is collected and see how the values change over time. The various elements are sampled and displayed, and you can also see a graph showing the values at each point at which an element was sampled. This graphical representation is especially good for pinpointing trends.

For example, if you right-click on SAMPLE and select Snapshot monitoring and Show monitor profiles you should see all the performance variables and their current values, if appropriate:

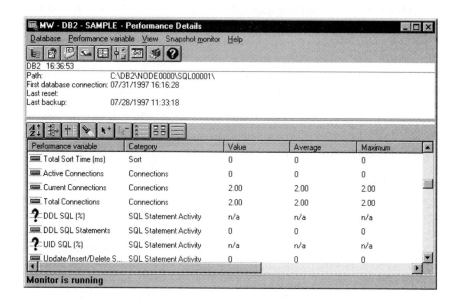

If you right-click on, say, total connections,

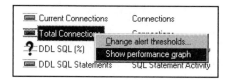

you can either change the alert thresholds (which takes you back to the monitor profile) or you can Show a performance graph, where you can watch how the values change with time.

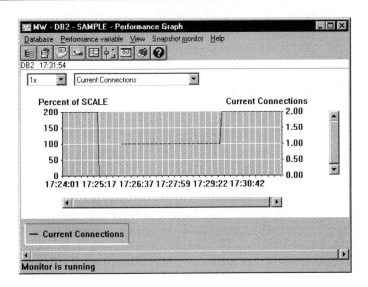

Here you can see the number of connections changing from 2 to 0 then back to 1 and finally 2.

The graph itself may look a little crude, but it can be configured and the important message is in the data.

❻ *As a final note, it is worth pointing out that you turn on monitoring for objects individually, but you can turn off all monitoring for an instance by right-clicking on its name and selecting Stop all monitoring.* ❾

*Chapter 15*

# Performance

DB2, as has been said already, is highly configurable. There are endless parameters to be tweaked, and if you right-click on a database in the object tree of the Control Center, select Configure and look at the Performance page, you can scroll through a list of just some of these.

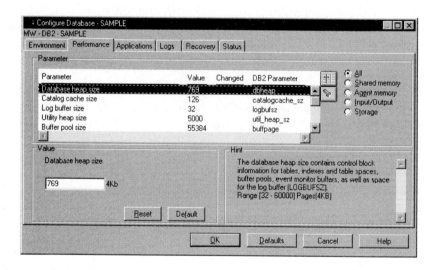

The high configurability is one factor giving DB2 its enormous power, but it also brings two disadvantages. One is that you need to know what you are doing to tweak parameters effectively, and the other is that these parameters have instantly forgettable names like *chngpgs_thresh* and *app_ctl_heap_sz*. Even if you guess that the latter is the application control heap size, you're no further towards knowing what a sensible value for it might be.

## The Performance SmartGuide

In this section we'll look at the Performance SmartGuide, which is, to a large extent, self-explanatory. We felt, however, that we couldn't ignore it because it is such a brilliant tool. IBM has done a great job of this SmartGuide; it's easy to use, the text is helpful, the default values sensible and the graphics are very attractive.

To launch this SmartGuide, right-click on a database object in the Control Center (we chose – you'll never guess – SAMPLE) and select Configure performance.

The first page of the SmartGuide is labeled Database, and here you can check that you've selected the correct database and change to another if you wish. It's worth reading the text for useful comments and general recommendations, such as this one saying that each instance should have only one production database.

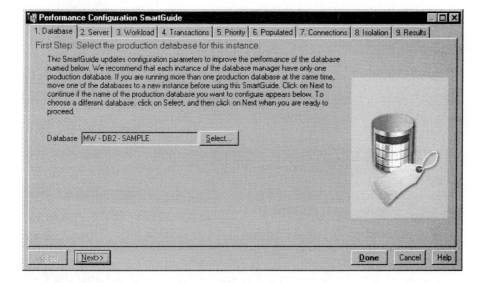

The Server page lets you set how much of the server's memory the database can use; if you have a dedicated server, you can set the slider to a high value. We've set ours to 80%. The page also reports the number of processors and identifies the operating system.

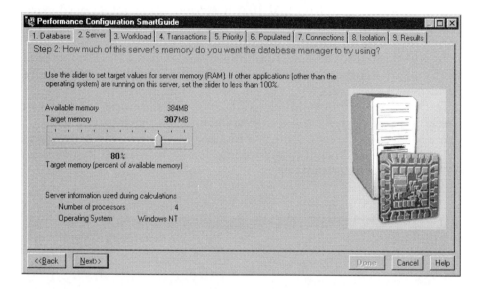

The Workload page lets you set the type of work your database usually does, and Mixed is a good default.

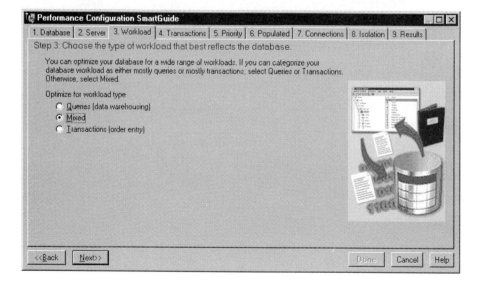

## 15 • Performance

The Transactions page essentially seeks information about how hard the database will work.

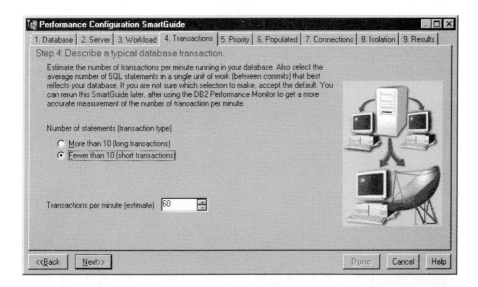

The Priority page asks you to choose between database speed and the speed of database recovery in the event of a problem.

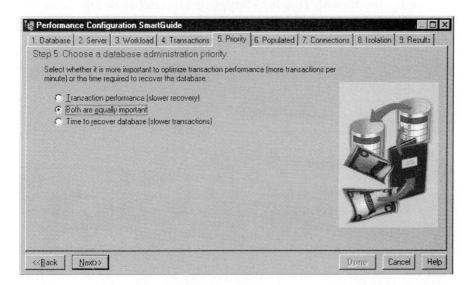

## 15 • Performance

Next (page 6) you can specify whether your database is populated with data. As the text says, you should run the SmartGuide again if there is a significant change in the size of the database.

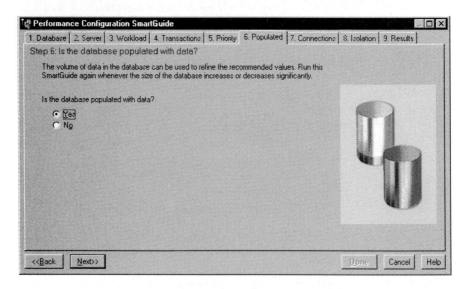

On the Connections page, specify the number of local and remote connections to the database. You don't have to get this right first time. You can always run the Snapshot Monitor later to obtain accurate information, rerun the SmartGuide and give it up-to-date values.

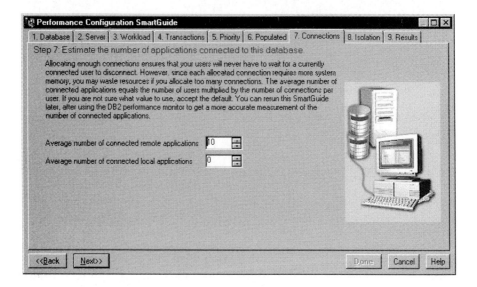

## 15 • Performance

This page is concerned with how an application uses the data in a database. When an application connects to the database, does it tend to lock a row and stop other users accessing that row for a considerable period, or does it just have a quick look?

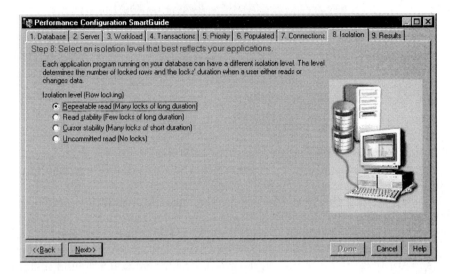

The last page, labeled Results, is the most important. It presents a list of decisions based on your input. Browsing these details is an excellent learning tool; for each, the full parameter name is shown in English, with its current value, the recommended value and finally the obscure parameter identifiers. At last we can translate *chngpgs_thresh*.

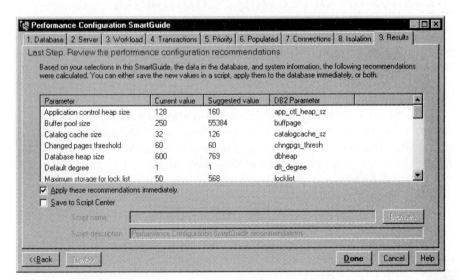

You can choose to apply the recommendations immediately; if you do, you'll see a message that you'll need to stop and restart the instance for the changes to take effect.

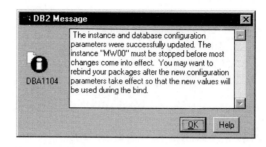

If you don't want to apply the recommendations now, you can save them to the Script Center or press Cancel to exit without changing anything.

That's it; that's the Performance SmartGuide. Its friendliness belies its importance and usefulness. You don't have to be an experienced DBA to use it: we suggest running it and looking at the values it suggests, and when things about the database change, running it again. Whether you decide to apply its recommendations or not, it will give you a deeper insight into DB2, and while there's no guarantee that a DBA with ten years' experience couldn't do better, it is certain that running the SmartGuide will give you better performance than using the defaults throughout.

## Statistics for Improving Performance

DB2 has a powerful performance optimizer that uses a set of statistics to determine the best methods for accessing data. If the data changes over time, these methods are also likely to change, and if DB2 does not have up-to-date statistics from which to determine those methods, performance will suffer.

So, to further improve performance, you should gather statistics about tables, columns and indexes from time to time, and DB2 provides a tool for doing this. The process of collecting statistics carries a performance overhead so, as ever, consider your database before gathering everything you can lay your hands on. Also, give serious consideration to using a script to schedule the process of data collection for the middle of the night.

To take a quick look at the Run Statistics dialog, right-click on a table name. Select Run Statistics from the menu.

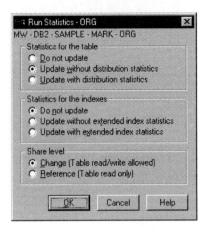

Radio buttons give control over the level of statistics you can collect for the tables and indexes, and further buttons set the access permitted to tables during the collection. The defaults are:

- to update the table statistics without distribution statistics;
- not to update the index statistics; and
- to permit read and write access to the table.

## Table Statistics

The statistics for the table can be updated either with or without distribution statistics. What, you might ask, are these? Statistics can be maintained about the distribution of values in a column, and the optimizer can make good use of this data to increase efficiency. As with all such tuning decisions, you must decide for your own data whether to use this option, weighing the extra loading against the efficiency gains.

The third option is not to update table statistics.

## Index Statistics

These can be updated either with or without extended index statistics. This simply determines the number of statistics gathered for an index, and the more details the optimizer has, the better it can optimize. As with table statistics, the decision whether to use the extended set can only be made by you for your data.

Again, the third option is not to update index statistics.

It is recommended that occasionally you collect table and index statistics at the same time to ensure that the two are synchronized.

## Share Level

The Change option gives other users read and write access to the table while statistics are being collected, and the Reference option means that they only have read access.

A number of the system tables are updated when you Run Statistics, including SYSCAT.TABLES and SYSSTAT.TABLES, SYSCAT.COLUMNS and SYSSTAT.COLUMNS and so on.

## Recommendations

Given a small database, don't bother. Given a database of any size, or one where the performance is beginning to become an issue, read up on the subject and start to collect statistics on a regular basis. Collect the information during idle time if possible and schedule the collection with a script.

*Chapter 16*

# Visual Explain Explained

Visual Explain is a tool that's used to dig deep into complex SQL statements, allowing you to see how DB2's optimizer is carrying them out. Given that information you may be able to tweak the process manually (perhaps by structuring your data differently) to make dilatory queries run more rapidly. We are really impressed by the power that this tool offers, but if you are just trying to get to grips with DB2 you really don't need to know about it yet. (*On the other hand, if you have had a stressful day and just want to play around with something that's good fun, go right ahead.*)

When you put Visual Explain to work on an SQL statement, you are shown a diagrammatic representation of the flow of data in the current access plan. Database objects and SQL operators are represented as various shapes on the screen (called nodes) and the flow of data between them as lines with arrowheads to indicate the direction in which data moves.

With Visual Explain you can inspect the details of:

- tables and indexes
- operators
- table spaces and functions

For example, you might discover that an index was not used by an access plan, which might lead you to define a more appropriate index producing performance gains.

## Visual Explain

Visual Explain presents a graphical view of a statement broken down into discrete steps showing the flow of data during its execution. It is a well-named tool, deserving both the 'Visual' part of its title and the 'Explain'. Curiously, it was present in DB2 before the present GUI-enhanced version.

## Access Plans

The efficiency with which an SQL statement is executed depends upon its access plan.

A single statement can be performed in many different ways, and as statements become more complex, the number of possible ways of performing them increases. Each possible path through the execution of a statement is called an access plan.

Imagine you have two tables, one containing employee records and one containing a record of the site at which each works, joined on employee number, and you simply want to know who works where. The SQL statement to generate this information could sort both tables into employee number order and locate like values, or it could look at each employee and pull out the relevant site details, or even look through the site records looking for a corresponding employee. These are all valid access plans, but some are more valid than others.

## Query Optimization

DB2 has built-in query optimization for determining the most efficient access plan, but, like all optimizers, it can benefit from occasional human help. This help takes the form of updating the statistics used by the optimizer. If a new index is added to a table, if many records are added to table, or if many have been updated, refreshing the statistics (as described in Chapter 15) lets the optimizer continue to work efficiently with the new data in the tables.

## Running Visual Explain

Right-click on a database (the long suffering SAMPLE again) and choose Explain SQL.

Type in an SQL statement, say:

```
Select id, name, deptname, division, location
From staff a, org b
Where a.dept = b.deptnumb
```

# 16 • Visual Explain Explained

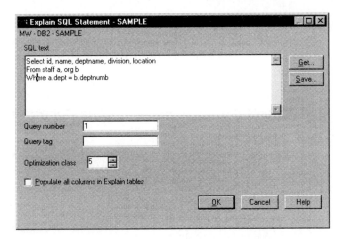

The setting for Optimization class is easy: the bigger the number, the better the optimization, though more time is spent on analysis. The Populate all columns option means save all of the information that's collected. Finally click on the OK button.

After a pause, the Access Plan graph should open up. We recommend that you choose View and Overview from the menu. This will open up the second window as shown:

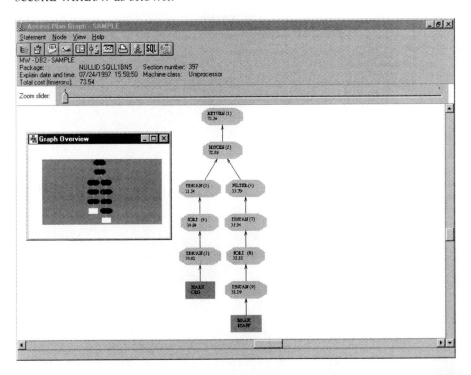

and you can use it to move around the access path and zoom in on interesting sections. As you can see below, the access path through a statement is like a string of beads, each bead being a node and the string equating to the path between them.

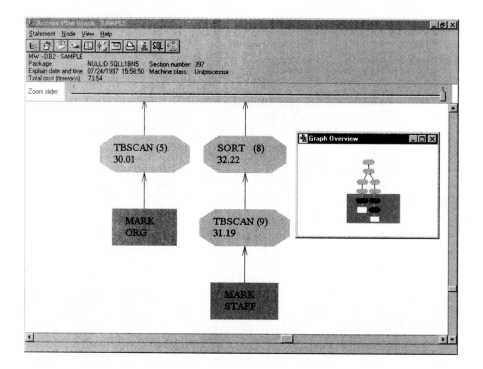

Double clicking on a node (in this case the Join) shows you further details

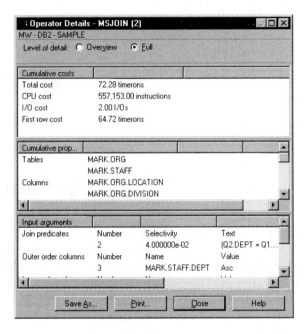

such as the number of CPU instructions (to two decimal places!). An estimated 'cost' for each operator is given in 'timerons', an arbitrary unit of measure (presumably as used by the Mysterons). The costs of different plans can be compared when working towards the most efficient solution.

The graphics can be displayed to read either from the bottom to the top of the screen, or from right to left (the direction of both seems counter-intuitive, but that's a minor criticism of a great tool).

When you first play with Visual Explain, start with a simple statement that you already fully understand. Once you see how it is represented, you are in a good position to use it to explain statements where your grasp is incomplete. You are unlikely to need to use Visual Explain in earnest until you are fairly well enmeshed with DB2, but knowing it's there is comforting.

❦ *The take-home message is 'You don't have to do this at home, kids... but it's a lot of fun'.*

Chapter 17

# Logs

DB2 maintains several log files that record various events, parameters, errors and so on. These can prove a useful source of information when you are grappling with a problem and all else fails. We say 'when all else fails' because these logs are written in a somewhat cryptic fashion and can be slow to divulge their secrets. However, it's worth a look because sometimes there can be just enough to give you a clue to the direction in which you should be heading.

For instance, a clatter of references to some particular parameter might be enough to prompt you to look more closely at the way it is set, and this could be enough to lead you to a solution.

The most useful log is:

```
C:\Sqllib\db2\db2diag.log
```

To inspect the log, simply use a text editor.

This log file just keep growing, so it's advisable to do a spot of housekeeping now and again. It is a simple text file, so it is easy to manipulate with a text editor (but see the warning below).

Other potentially useful log/configuration files are:

```
C:\Sqllib\db2cfg.txt
C:\Sqllib\db2cli.ini
C:\Sqllib\db2clias.lst
C:\WINNT\Odbcinst.ini
C:\WINNT\Odbc.ini
```

Our advice is look, but don't touch unless you know what you are doing. If you do touch, take a backup first, just in case.

*Chapter 18*

# Relational Extenders

There is a range of new features in DB2; not necessarily new to Version 5, but new in terms of general database functionality. You may have heard the terms already, and the descriptions below should help put them in context. We don't cover how to use these features, as they are well outside 'get you going quickly' territory, but an overview may be a useful addition to your knowledge base.

## Extended Data Types

Relational extenders extend the relational model, and the relational model needs extending because it was built to handle what can be termed 'structured data' – text, numbers, binary numbers etc. Progress marches on, and we now see an increasing need to handle unstructured data, such as images and video and audio data.

There are two distinct differences with unstructured data. Firstly, it has new and different attributes; a video clip, for example, has attributes like number of frames, duration, format and so on. These attributes cannot be addressed by existing functions; returning the first four characters of a text string has no meaning when applied to a video clip. It is also clear that different functions are required, ones to return the first twenty frames, or to locate the 155th frame, for instance.

Secondly, the data has a potential behavior that means it must be handled in a specialized way; you need to be able to play video and audio clips, and to view images.

DB2's relational extenders encapsulate the attributes and behavior of unstructured data types, allowing them to reside in columns and be handled with the same ease as more usual types of data.

## User-Defined Distinct Types

When building a database, it is sometimes helpful to be able to limit the values in a column. While this is possible using business rules and triggers, it can be done at an even more fundamental level by defining a new data type. These new types are called user-defined distinct types, and are known, not surprisingly, as UDTs.

If your business sells goods in two countries, you would expect your database to hold entries in various tables in different currencies, perhaps French francs and Canadian dollars. Columns containing such values could happily be declared to be of type decimal. Problems could arise, however, when users tried to add or compare prices: a value from a francs column could happily be added to one from a dollars column, and the user could be blissfully unaware that the answer was complete nonsense.

Using UDTs can stop even sillier sorts of computations, such as adding a duration in minutes and seconds to a sum of money, or someone's hat size to their shoe size.

If two new distinct types were declared, one for prices in francs and one for dollars, such computations could not be performed. The types are distinct, and therefore incompatible for comparison or arithmetical operations.

The use of UDTs goes some way towards the implementation of domains. Simplistically speaking, this is the process of ensuring that only values taken from pools of data of the same type can be compared, summed or whatever. (For more about domains, read *Inside Relational Databases* as mentioned in the introduction.)

A UDT is based on an existing data type; in the example above you would start with the data type Decimal and alter its definition to suit your needs.

For those who like knowing such things, all data types, including UDTs, are listed in the SYSDATATYPES table.

## User-Defined Functions

There are occasions when users wish to perform data manipulations which are not easily supported by DB2's in-built functions, and it is then that the user-defined function (UDF) comes into its own. Being able to define purpose-built functions gives an extremely high level of flexibility for manipulating data.

DB2's range of built-in functions is comprehensive and can be classified into three types:

- arithmetic and string operators (+, −, /, * etc.)
- scalar functions (length, days, etc.)
- column functions (avg, count, min, max etc.)

There are two types of user-defined function:

- sourced functions
- external functions

A sourced function is based on an existing built-in function, which is known as its 'source function'. The behavior of a source function is inherited by the sourced function, offering an efficient way of creating a new function with some of its properties ready-made.

An external function is written in C or C++ and can carry out any computations on the parameters passed to it, though such functions are not permitted to access or modify the database.

User-defined functions are always created in a specific database and can be used only within that database, and all such functions are stored in the tables SYSFUNCTIONS and SYSFUNCPARMS.

*Chapter 19*

# Test Data

When playing around with a new RDBMS, we often want to generate large sets of test data. This can be done in many ways, but two methods are typically employed.

- You can generate the data using a PC RDBMS like Access and import it into DB2.
- You can us a PC RDBMS to drive DB2 and get DB2 to generate the data.

The former is often faster, while the latter is easier because you don't have to import the data (although data import in DB2 is easy anyway).

## Generation Within Access

We use a set of routines that I (Mark) wrote in Access several years ago. In fact these were written originally for a magazine called *PC User* in the UK. The magazine wanted a large test database filled with 'reasonably realistic' data so I wrote some code and 'seed' data in Access. Using these it is possible to generate files of essentially unlimited size. The publishing house which owned *PC User*, emap, has kindly agreed to allow us to include the code and sample tables on the CD-ROM.

Jonny Black (see Acknowledgements) tidied up my rather ratty code, and it is included in subdirectories underneath `D:\DB24NTF`. If you use it, and want to get the data into DB2, you will have to export it from Access and import it into DB2 via some sort of intermediate file format.

## Generation Using a Front-End to Drive DB2

We felt rather mean about providing an Access-specific tool (what about all the people who don't use Access?) so Jonny also wrote an Approach tool which manipulates DB2 and gets it to generate the data. That is also provided on the CD-ROM.

As with all of the other stuff we provide, this comes with no guarantees, but a whole raft of warnings. We don't know if it will work on your system; we assume that you are reasonably competent with either Access or Approach; please be careful; we aren't providing support or help but there are READMEs. Having said all of that, we have tested both and they seem to work fine. If they don't work for you, at least you have some code that you can modify.

## Importing, Exporting and Loading Data

DB2 offers two methods of filling your tables with data, Import and Load.

The Import utility is used to move data from a table/view into another database or between DB2 databases, and the data to be imported can be located on a client. Importing data is the slow option because each row is added as an SQL insert operation, each addition is fully logged, all constraints validated and all triggers fired.

Import is available simply by right-clicking on the table name, selecting Import, and following the directions in the dialog boxes. (*To no one's great surprise, export is available from the same menu by selecting Export.*)

Load, on the other hand, is quick and is the more suitable utility when large amounts of data are to be moved. The data to be moved must be local to the server. Load writes formatted pages directly into the database, rather than writing them a row at a time. Minimal logs are kept, triggers are not supported and only unique constraints are checked.

❖ *When we say 'Minimal logs are kept' what we really mean is that a record that the load took place is put in the transaction log, nothing else. So you are well advised to set in place some recovery plan in case an earlier backup is restored and rolled forward past the load point.* ❖

# Index

**A**
Access  42, 234
  configuring as front-end  70, 73–4
access profiles  59
  generating  60
Alert Center  96, 100–1
alias  52, 58, 62, 65
Approach  42
  configuring as front-end  74, 79
authorities  12, 143–53
  database-level  144
  DBADM  150
  granting  145, 149, 152
  groups and  148
  instance-level  144
  types of  144
  *see also* privileges
authority, used to mean 'privilege'  147
automatic startup  27
autostart  15
  Control Center  46

**B**
back-end  1
backup  167–86
  configuring  184–5
  defined  167
  to disk  171
  location of  171
  off-line  167, 183
  on-line  167, 183
  reasons for  175–6
  scheduled  172
  script  172
  strategy  181–3, 185
  to tape  171, 173
business rules  136
  triggers and  191

**C**
CAE *see* Client Application Enabler
Cascade Delete  130, 134
CCA *see* Client Configuration Assistant
Client Application Enabler  13, 43
  installation  45
Client Configuration Assistant  43
  server  64, 67
  workstation  48, 63
client–server  1
client workstation  83–8
  connecting to DB2  84
Command Center  18, 20, 25, 96, 98
  Results tab  23
  Script tab  20
Command Line Processor  93
  Command Window and  96
  exiting  95
Command Window  93, 95
  Command Line Processor and  96
communications protocols  15–16
  TCP/IP  15
configuration files  230
constraints  126
  check  134, 136, 138, 161
    creating  137
    multiple  137
  loading data and  235
  NOT NULL  134–5
  primary  126
  types of  134
  unique  134–5
containers  104, 106, 109, 112
  adding  125
  choosing  123
  creating  116–17
  large databases  114
  overview  105
  reasons for using  114
  small databases  114
  types of  109, 113
Control Center  28–38, 96–7
  autostart  46
  contents pane  28
  creating databases  115

# Index

Databases 30–1
  filters 32
  Force applications 168
  Indexes 132
  Instances 29–30
  object tree 28
  running 28
  Systems 29
  table spaces and 107, 122
  toolbars 29
  Views 160
coverage of book 3

## D
data
  deleting 133–4
  entry 133
  exporting 235
  importing 235
  loading 235
  manipulating 81–2
  sorting 138
  test *see* test data
  value of 175
data entry, errors 126
data types
  audio 231
  extended 231
  long 111
  user-defined distinct types 232
  video 231
DataBase Administrator 2
Database Administrator Authority *see* DBADM
Database Managed Space 109, 113, 122
  types of 110
databases
  adding 49
    access profiles 50, 59, 63
    manual configuration 50, 54, 59
    searching the network 49–50, 54
  adding description 68
  connecting to 21, 65
  containers *see* containers
  creating 34–6, 104–25
  large 114
  restoring *see* restore
  size of 114
  small 114
DB2 1
  defined 1
  historical background 104
  monitoring 201–15
  tools *see* tools
  tuning 104
DBA *see* DataBase Administrator
DBADM 2, 144, 146
  abilities 146
Delphi 42, 83–5, 88
  configuring as front-end 79, 81
DMS *see* Database Managed Space
DOS prompt *see* Command Window

## E
Event Analyzer 96, 101, 201
Event Monitor *see* event monitoring
event monitoring 90–1, 101, 201–2
  database connections 202, 205
  deadlock activity 202, 207
  files created 205
  filters 202
  number of monitors 207
  setting up 202
  SQL statements 202, 207
  transactions 202, 206
  viewing files 205
extent size 119

## F
filters 32, 120
First Steps 18, 92
foreign keys 19, 126
  adding 127, 130, 132
  indexes and 139
front-end 1
  capabilities of 74
  choosing 42
  configuring for ODBC 70
  connecting to database 133
  creating an application 83
  DB2 setup 43–4, 48
  installation plan 40
  installing 39–82
  manipulating data 81
  overview 39
  sample applications 84
  SQL and 81
  target database 57
  testing connection 53
  types of 42
  user ID 53
functions
  external 233
  sourced 233

# Index

user-defined  232, 233

## G
groups  143
  names  149
  NT  148–9
  privileges and  144
  public  147
  PUBLIC  143

## H
hardware  5–6
  crash  177

## I
indexes  126–40
  constraints and  135
  containers and  114
  creating  140
  deciding what to index  139
  disadvantages  139
  foreign keys and  139
  optimizing  139
  primary keys and  139
  reasons for using  138
  statistics  223
  table spaces and  112–14
  using  138
Information Center  96, 102–3
*Inside Relational Databases*  2
installation  11–27
  custom  14
  directories created  25
  log file  26, 47
  on NT Server  11
  selecting products to install  13
  types of  13–14
instances  29–30
integrity  126–40
  triggers and  191

## J
Java  83–4, 88
jobs  100
Journal  96, 100, 172

## L
layout of book  5
log files  178, 230
  active  178
  archiving and  180
  backing up  182
  contents of  179
  location of  181–2
  number of  185
  primary  178
  secondary  178
  size of  185
  SQL and  179
logging
  archive  180, 182
  circular  178–9, 181
    advantages and disadvantages  179–80
logs  174, 177, 230
  loading data  235
  multiple  178
  on- and off-line  181
  *see also* logging

## M
manipulating data, front-end  82

## N
NetBIOS  47
null values  128

## O
objects  34
  dropping  155
  naming  155–6
ODBC  40
  configuring front-end  70
  data source  40, 48
    configuring  67, 69
    properties  67
    registering  52, 58, 65
optimization  115

## P
password  16–17, 53, 65, 68
  Access  72
  ODBC  68–9
performance  114, 125, 138, 216–24
  connections  220
  memory  218
  priority  219
  scripts  222
  small databases  224
  statistics  222
  transactions  219
  workload  218
permissions  159
point-in-time recovery  180
prefetch size  119

# Index

primary keys  19, 73, 78, 126
  adding  128–30
  indexes and  129, 132, 139
privileges  11–12, 143–53
  automatic  147
  CONNECT  147
  CONTROL  147–8
  CREATETAB  147
  defined  146
  granting  145, 152–3
  individuals and  148
  table and view  147
  types of  147
  *see also* authorities
programming languages  84
prune history  186–8

## Q
queries  163
  frequent  114
  indexes and  139
  optimizing  226

## R
RDBMS  1
readership  1
recovery  167–85
referential integrity  74, 126
relational extenders  231–3
restore  173, 175
  Restore Database Recovery History  183
rollback  177, 179
  automatic  182
roll forward  174, 180
  pending state  183–4

## S
sample applications  84
  limitations of  85–6
SAMPLE database  18–19
  containers  110
  tables  19
  table spaces  110
  testing  20
sample files  83
saving data, Database Managed Space *see* System Managed Space
scheduling  186–90
  reasons for  186
schemas  76, 154–8, 165–6
  creating  154
  naming  154
  reasons for using  155–6
  referencing tables  156
  using  156
Script Center  96, 99
scripts  20–1, 23–4, 98–9, 186
  creating  187
  prune history  99
  scheduling  186–7, 190
  SmartGuides and  99
server
  hostname  55
  NetWare  41
  port number  15, 56–7
  secure  41
  working from  40–2
services  26–7
share level  224
SmartGuides  34, 36
  Add Database  49
  Backup  173
  Backup Database  168, 182
  Create Database  35, 116
  Create Table  36–8
  Performance  217–22
  Restore  173
  scripts and  99
SMS *see* System Managed Space
Snapshot Monitor *see* snapshot monitoring
snapshot monitoring  90, 100, 207, 220
  alarm thresholds  212
  Alert Center  213
  database connections  209
  graphs  213–15
  interval  212
  number of rows read per second  209, 211
  scripts and  211
  Show monitor details  208
  Show monitoring profile  208, 213
  Start monitoring  208, 213
  Stop monitoring  208
speed *see* performance
SQL  22
  front-end and  81
  generating  164–5
  log files and  179
  schemas and  158
  triggers and  191
  views and  160, 162
  Visual Explain and  225

# Index

statistics  222, 224
storage, types of  109
SYSADM  2, 11–12, 144–5, 148
  abilities  145
SYSCTRL  144–6
  abilities  145
  compared with SYSADM  145
SYSMAINT  144, 146
  abilities  146
System Administration Authority
  see SYSADM
System Control Authority
  see SYSCTRL
System Maintenance Authority
  see SYSMAINT
System Managed Space  109, 111, 113
system tables  31

## T
tables  112
  catalog  120
  containers and  105
  creating  36–8, 104–25
  in multiple containers  106
  multiple table spaces  112
  naming  155
  size of  119
  statistics  223
  system  224
  table spaces and see table spaces
table spaces  104, 111–12
  in Control Center  107
  created by SmartGuide  121
  large databases  114
  Long  111–12, 122
  Long data  124
  multiple containers and  115
  overview  105–7, 109
  reasons for using  114
  Regular  111–12
  rules  106
  small databases  114
  Temporary  111
  types of  111–12
TCP/IP  55
test data  234–5
  generating using front-end  234–5
  generating with Access  234
timerons  229
tools  89–103
  Alert Center  96, 100–1
  Certification  93
  Client Configuration Assistant  43
  Command Center  18, 20, 25, 46, 98
  Command Line Processor  93
  Command Window  93, 95
  Control Center  28–38, 96–7
  Event Analyzer  96, 101, 201
  Event Monitor  89
  First Steps  18, 92
  grouping of  92
  iconed  91
  Information Center  96, 102–3
  Journal  96, 100, 172
  location of icons  92
  most important  103
  non-iconed  89
  Release Notes  93
  Script Center  96, 99
  Snapshot Monitor  89
  Support through Internet  93
  Tools Settings  96, 101
  Trace Utility  92
  Uninstall  92
Tools Settings  96, 101
Trace Utility  92
transactions  176–8
  committed  176
  importance of  177
  incomplete  176
  rollback  177
  uncommitted  180
triggers  81, 191–8
  activation time  192
  After  192–3
  Before  192–3
  body  193
  conditions  193, 196
  creating  194–5
  defined  191
  DELETE  192
  granularity  192
  INSERT  192
  loading data and  235
  names  191
  restrictions  192–3
  Row  192
  SQL and  191
  SQL template  195
  Statement  192–3
  tables and  193
  terminology  191–2
  UPDATE  192

# Index

**U**
UDF *see* functions, user-defined
UDT *see* data types, user-defined distinct types
Uninstall  92
user ID  65, 68
  Access  72
  ODBC  68–9
username  16–17, 65
  restrictions on  11
users  143–53
  groups and  143–4

**V**
versioning  4
views  159–66
  compared with queries  163
  creating  160, 163
  multiple tables  163, 166
  naming  160
  reasons for using  159
  SQL and  160
  updateable  163
  as virtual tables  163
VisualAge for Basic  83–4, 87
Visual Basic  83–6
Visual Explain  225–9
  access plans  226–7
  functions of  225
  running  226

**W**
Welcome dialog  12
Windows NT  11
workstation
  client *see* client workstation
  front-end installation  44
  working from  40–1